A typical scene in Restoration comedy, taken from a 1761 edition of Vanbrugh's *The Provok'd Wife*. *Courtesy of The Pennsylvania State University Library*

CRITICS, VALUES, AND RESTORATION COMEDY

JOHN T. HARWOOD

SOUTHERN ILLINOIS UNIVERSITY PRESS
Carbondale and Edwardsville

Copyright © 1982 by the Board of Trustees, Southern Illinois
University
All rights reserved
Printed in the United States of America
Edited by Stephen W. Smith
Designed by Quentin Fiore

Library of Congress Cataloging in Publication Data
Harwood, John T.
  Critics, values, and Restoration comedy.

  Bibliography: p.
  Includes index.
    1. English drama—Restoration, 1660–1700—History
and criticism.   2. English drama (Comedy)—History and
criticism.   3. Literature and morals.   4. Criticism.
I. Title.
PR698.C6H3   1982   822'.0523   81-18397
ISBN 0-8093-1049-X   AACR2

For Elizabeth and Benjamin

Contents

Preface	ix
1. "This lubrique and adult'rate age": The Attacks on Restoration Comedy	1
2. "The Usefulness of the Stage": Restoration Comedy *Moralisé* and the *Réaliste* Tradition	10
3. "Escape from this dull age": The *Artificielle* Tradition	35
4. Literature and Moral Persuasion: The Critics' Dilemma	50
5. "Deep-Breathing Sex" and Critical Practice	77
6. "Duels, Claps, and Bastards": The Problem of Sympathy and Judgment	115
Notes	145
Selected Bibliography	163
Index	175

Preface

Restoration comedy has been a bête noire for literary critics and historians for several centuries. No other literature seems as likely to propel its critics either into paroxysms of moral indignation or rhapsodies of lyrical praise. The vigorous and contentious dispute about the moral issues raised by the comedies is especially interesting, for in the last three centuries critics have argued vehemently for or against such diverse theses as: 1) Restoration comedy exposes the reader to the infectious disease of moral turpitude with which the dramatis personae are terminally ill; 2) Restoration comedy is entertaining (or boring) but nothing more; 3) Restoration comedy is a bracing tonic, a healthful and stimulating criticism of sterile and repressive social conventions; 4) Restoration comedy allows the reader to enter a rarefied world of gallantry and rococo manners—such an escape from the mundane world is salutary; and 5) Restoration comedy is a treasure chest for the historian who wants an accurate picture of late seventeenth-century social conditions, values, and mores in England. The first four theses pertain directly to the moral effect of imaginative literature, in this case Restoration comedy, on the reader; the fifth attempts to avoid the moral issue by focusing entirely on the sociological and historical relation of drama and society, though few of these "neutral" critics can avoid waffling on the moral issue. But despite the abundance of moral judgments about the comedy, no critic has examined closely the critical and moral assumptions behind other critics' ethical responses or, more broadly, has analyzed thoroughly the assumptions behind an ethical judgment of literature. A need exists, therefore, for a clarification of the critical presuppositions of the major critics of Restoration comedy and particularly of the criticism in which moral judgments are inextricably embedded in the critical commentary.

My purpose is not as polemical as the redoubtable Mr. Bateson's, who concludes a survey of modern critics thus: "all lively and all wrong."[1] My thesis has three broad interests: first, I survey the major rhetorical strategies by which many "objective" critics transform themselves, at least momentarily and perhaps unconsciously, into moralistic critics when they deal with Restoration comedy. Second, I consider the various moral responses in a broader critical context by analyzing how critics have traditionally handled the aesthetic problems which an ethical evaluation of literature inevitably entails. And third, I analyze in some detail the moral dimensions of four controversial Restoration comedies, each presenting different moral visions and critical problems. While my essay begins with a survey of the critical responses to Restoration comedy, its ultimate concern is with a question posed by Santayana some years ago, a question that reflects on the value of all imaginative literature. "It is in the world, however, that art must find its level. It must vindicate its function in the human commonwealth. What direct acceptable contribution does it make to the highest good?"[2]

Such a study could swell to Brobdingnagian proportions if I did not impose certain restrictions on its scope and methodology. First, for the sake of clarity I will categorize the critics on the basis of their assumptions about Restoration comedy rather than follow the kind of chronological approach which leads Earl Miner to mar an otherwise cogent essay with shaky historical generalizations. "Restoration critics charged [the comedy] with profanity in the strict sense; eighteenth and nineteenth century critics found it guilty of sexual license. . . . Modern traducers of Restoration comedy have sophisticated the charge into one of sterile preoccupation with sex."[3] Miner's statements need qualification: though John Wain would undoubtedly deny his similarity to Collier and Macaulay, his work, as I will show, resembles theirs in several respects.

Preface

Furthermore, I will not discuss in much detail several of the most popular errors which appear in the criticism. For example, most critics persist in using "Restoration comedy" as a generic label, failing to differentiate among clearly identifiable kinds of comic drama. In 1923 Allardyce Nicoll described seven different types in *A History of Restoration Drama*,[4] and more recently A. H. Scouten and Robert D. Hume[5] have analyzed and categorized more precisely the distinct types of comedies which appeared after 1660. The work of these scholars suggests that "Restoration comedy" has no clear and unambiguous referent; to characterize Shadwell's *The Virtuoso*, Ravenscroft's *The London Cuckolds*, and Congreve's *The Way of the World* as "Restoration comedies" designates nothing but a rough time reference and ignores substantial differences among the plays. However tempting it is for critics to generalize about a static "Restoration comedy," one must realize that "Restoration comedy" is nearly as informative a label for the comic drama as the "Age of Reason" for eighteenth-century literature.

A more serious error is the tendency to commingle judgments of Restoration comedy and Restoration society. While critics may be enamored of or repelled by their conceptions of Restoration society, they should not allow their evaluations of the plays to be tinctured by their attitudes toward that society. Such critics usually read Anthony Hamilton's *The Memoirs of Count Grammont* as an infallible guide to Restoration social history, producing criticism like this: "The Restoration was the most licentious, wicked, and bawdy era in English history, and the comedies are an accurate reflection of the decadence of the audience." There are at least two things wrong with this view. First, there is no historical evidence to indicate that there was more sexual license during the Restoration than in other periods. Indeed, Peter Laslett's demographic study of the percentage of illegitimate births and of brides who bore a child within nine months of marriage indicates that sexual promiscuity, so far as it is measurable by these categories, was lower in the Restoration than in the 1590s and the mid-eighteenth century.[6] The facile equation of a lubricious society and a decadent drama should be destroyed when one half of the equation is removed. This easy congruence of a debased society and drama fits neatly into the Whig interpretation of history but apparently has no basis in fact.

A corollary of this point is also worth mentioning. Restoration dramatists are not sociologists, though some critics treat the comedies as sociological treatises and the dramatists as forerunners of Margaret Mead and Vance Packard. Several decades ago Elmer Stoll argued vigorously against this practice, and perhaps just one sentence can put the matter into an accurate perspective. "Literature," he writes, "reflects the taste of the time rather than the time itself, and often the two are widely different."[7] To make Restoration comedy into sociological textbooks is to force Calliope onto Procrustes' bed: though many Restoration comedies have elements of bedroom farce, such bedroom tussling is inappropriate in criticism. While numerous nineteenth-century critics abhorred the drama because of the society which they thought was mirrored in the plays, some modern critics commit the same fallacy because they admire the society—or what they *imagine* to have been Restoration society—reflected in the comedies. It is more than ironic that both groups of critics, the "libertines" and the "prigs," find themselves cheek-to-cheek on this matter.

Nor will I be concerned with the criticism of particular plays or authors, though I will refer occasionally to it. Most critics of particular plays or authors cannot resist the temptation to generalize and to moralize about other plays; their broadest statements about art are most revelatory of their critical assumptions and thus most relevant to my study.

Finally, I will not attempt to reconstruct the historical context from which much criticism derives at least some of its meaning. That is, to understand John Dennis's defense of *The Man of Mode* in 1722, it is helpful to consider not only Dennis's literary principles but his personal antipathy toward Sir Richard Steele, who had attacked the play. Many critics are responding not only to particular works but to their age (what Eliot and Arnold would call their Culture) as well. To present more than a glimpse of the

Preface

historical milieux which shape the critical voices I will consider is beyond the scope of this study. Rather than chronicle the ephemeral and personal controversies intertwined with critical disputes, I will survey in the first part of this essay the main lines of attack on Restoration comedy and then present in its various forms the responses to this attack, the *moralisé* tradition.

In chapters five and six I look closely at the moral visions of four comedies, each popular with it original audience. My critical approach to *The London Cuckolds, The Country Wife, The Souldiers Fortune,* and *The Squire of Alsatia* investigates conventions of comic drama that comment on and endorse ideas and values, especially conventions through which the audience is invited to judge the validity of general propositions tested by the dramatic action of the plays. These comedies raise different kinds of questions. *The London Cuckolds* and *The Country Wife* are particularly concerned with questions of sexual politics, to use Kate Millett's phrase, and I am interested in the techniques by which Ravenscroft and Wycherley shape the response of the audience to their characters' sexual adventures. *The Souldiers Fortune* (and its sequel, *The Atheist*) offers a grimly pessimistic view of justice and human relationships. In such a world, Otway affirms only male friendship and drinking. *The Squire of Alsatia* is an "education" play, testing the values by which a young gentleman ought to live and illustrating the perils of raising a young man to maturity. I deal with Otway and Shadwell because they raise ethical questions not necessarily related to sexual conduct. I conclude by placing in broader perspective the critical questions and methodological problems central to this study. In essence, then, this study examines an ancient and significant literary quarrel that has found a particularly vigorous expression in the debate about Restoration comedy during the last three centuries. At issue is the question of *instruction*. Beyond a doubt, literature delights; in what way, though, does it teach? How do beliefs about its effects on audiences shape critics' responses to and judgment of literature? Does literature achieve those effects? How do we know?

Preface

WITHOUT A SUBSTANTIAL BODY OF LIVELY CRITICISM, ancient and modern, I would not have begun this study, and I am indebted to all of the critics from whom I learned. I have also learned from colleagues who criticized early versions of my study: Robert D. Stock, Howard Norland, and Frederick M. Link were especially helpful. Alice F. Randall and Thomas J. Musial helped me define theoretical questions more precisely; Robert D. Hume and Judith Milhous made numerous suggestions that clarified my argument. Calhoun Winton, Charles Mann, Douglas Butler, and Stephen Smith contributed assistance that only each could have provided. Margie Simmons and Nancy Royer provided expert typing under difficult conditions.

With such generous assistance from so many colleagues, I might reasonably expect that all present and future critics would accept all my conclusions. Modesty requires me to admit, however, that not one of my colleagues is fully persuaded by all parts of my argument, partly because of the nature of my argument and partly because of the nature of the problems I address.

JOHN T. HARWOOD

The Pennsylvania State University
University Park, Pennsylvania
September 1981

CRITICS, VALUES, AND RESTORATION COMEDY

February 9, 1668. Up, and at my chamber all the morning and the office, doing business and also reading a little of *L'escolle des Filles*, which is a mighty lewd book, but yet not amiss for a sober man once to read over to inform himself in the villainy of the world. . . . We sang till almost night, and drank my good store of wine; and then they parted and I to my chamber, where I did read through *L'escholle des Filles*; a lewd book, but what doeth me no wrong to read for information sake (But it did hazer my prick para stand all the while, and una vez to decharger); and after I had done it, I burned it, that it might not be among my books to my shame; and so at night to supper and then to bed. (*The Diary of Samuel Pepys*)

Poetry . . . should offer a means of enriching one's awareness of human experience and of so rendering greater the possibility of intelligence in the course of future action; and it should offer likewise a means of inducing certain more or less constant habits of feeling, which should render greater the possibility of one's acting, in a future situation, in accordance with the findings of one's improved intelligence and strengthen the moral temper; . . . If the poetic discipline is to have steadiness and direction, it requires an antecedent discipline of ethical thinking and of at least some ethical feeling, which may be in whole or in part the gift of religion or of a social tradition, or which may be largely the result of individual acquisition by way of study. (Yvor Winters, *Primitivism and Decadence*)

The highest, as the lowest, form of criticism is a mode of autobiography. Those who find ugly meanings in beautiful things are corrupt without being charming. This is a fault. Those who find beautiful meanings in beautiful things are the cultivated. For these there is hope. They are the elect to whom beautiful things mean only Beauty. There is no such thing as a moral or an immoral book. Books are well written, or badly written. That is all. . . . No artist has ethical sympathies. An ethical sympathy in an artist is an unpardonable mannerism of style. . . . We can forgive a man for making a useful thing as long as he does not admire it. The only excuse for making a useless thing is that one admires it intensely. All art is quite useless. (Oscar Wilde, Preface to *The Picture of Dorian Gray*)

1

"This lubrique and adult'rate age": The Attacks on Restoration Comedy

It was once fashionable to say that romanticism erupted in 1798 because the *Lyrical Ballads* were published in that year. In a similar vein of literary history, the "immorality and profaneness" of the Restoration stage supposedly were expunged in 1698 by that nonjuring Jacobite, Jeremy Collier, whose *A Short View of the Immorality and Profaneness of the English Stage* helped to establish the "weeping comedy" as the dominant form of eighteenth-century comedy. Such notions about literary history are, of course, untenable if one is interested in *facts* about the changes in dramatic form and critical sensibility. Collier's *Short View*, brief only in comparison to similar attacks on the stage by such earlier critics as William Prynne (*Histrio-Mastix*, 1633), is but one of many seventeenth-century attempts to abolish, not reform, the stage. (Collier initially denied but later admitted that he was more interested in abolition than in reformation.) Collier proudly proclaims the pedigree of his argument by citing the "authorities," chiefly patristic, in the fifth part of his "short view" when he rhetorically allies himself, as Pope was to do in *An Essay on Criticism* (1711), with critics whose views he finds most congenial and correct. Collier's attack has been maligned, I suspect, more often than read, but the furious clergyman should be given his due: he is devilishly clever, witty, learned, and adept at argumentation. He is also perverse (wrenching "smut" out of very ordinary dialogue), unbalanced (he seems to weigh violations of "poetic justice" and of "the unities" equally), and confused about the rela-

CRITICS, VALUES, AND RESTORATION COMEDY

tion of the writer and his dramatis personae (typical of his method is to hold that every statement of every character represents the author's position on a particular issue). His importance to this study is his assertion that drama has a moral purpose, restating for the seventeenth century the Aristotelian-Horatian synthesis found earlier in Sir Philip Sidney's *Defense of Poesy* and elsewhere. "The business of *Plays* is to recommend Virtue, and discountenance Vice; to shew the Uncertainty of Humane greatness, the suddain Turns of Fate, and the Unhappy Conclusions of Violence and Injustice: 'Tis to expose the Singularities of Pride and Fancy, to make Folly and Falsehood contemptible, and to bring every Thing that is Ill Under Infamy, and Neglect."[1]

Restoration comedies, Collier says, have forsaken their didactic function and have become infamous for "their *Smuttiness* of *Expression*," "their *Swearing, Profaneness,* and *Lewd Application of Scripture*," "their *Abuse* of the *Clergy*," and "their *making* their top *Characters Libertines*, and giving them Success in their Debauchery." The witty persiflage of rakes and witty virgins is merely licentious discourse that "tends to no point but to stain the Imagination, to awaken Folly, and to weaken the Defences of Virtue"; and, he continues, "'tis not safe for a man to trust his virtue too far, for fear it should give him the slip" (pp. 5–6). The "ethos" endorsed by Restoration heroes is succinctly characterized by Collier's definition of "the fine Gentleman" as a "fine Whoring, Swearing, Smutty, Atheistical Man" (p. 143). Firing random salvos at *Absalom and Achitophel* ("Here are no Pagan Divinities in the Scheme, so that all the Atheistick Raillery must point upon the true God") and countless plays, Collier implicitly blames the stage for infecting the age with its spurious moral values instead of inculcating virtue. And though opponents of the theatre from Gosson to Collier had warned that "unsavory" women frequented the theatre (one recalls Pepys's apparent delight at being spat upon by a "very pretty woman" in the pit), Collier notices not only their debasing presence but seizes upon another source of corruption which had seldom been touched on since Plato: music, he says, was nearly as treacherous as the plays and their unsavory audiences. "Now why should it be in the power of a few

The Attacks on Restoration Comedy

mercenary Hands to play People out of their Senses, to run away with their Understandings, and wind their Passions about their Fingers as they list? Musick is almost as dangerous as Gunpowder; And it may be requires looking after no less than the Press, or the Mint. 'Tis possible a Publick Regulation might not be amiss" (p. 279). Collier's omnibus indictment, in brief, argues heatedly that the theatre corrupts because of its "atmosphere," vile language, misdirected ridicule, and because "the Stage-Poets make their Principal Persons Vitious, and reward them at the End of the Play." Even if the plays mirror the moral deformities of the age, they do nothing to correct them, and it is most likely that they fomented the vices they mirror. Collier observed his society and its entertainment and saw, in Dryden's words at the end of the century, a "lubrique and adult'rate age."

Collier's strictures on Restoration comedy have been elaborated at some length because they evaluate literature by a moral criterion, describe what the criterion is, and include nearly all the arguments and critical tactics which have been used to deprecate the plays, their authors, and Restoration society by subsequent critics. While later critics have not always been as lucid in presenting the moral measure by which they evaluate the plays, they have still used Collier's arguments. Adverse criticism nearly always sweeps the plays, authors, and society into the same sickroom, murmuring that they are, in Dryden's famous lament for his age, "all, all of a piece throughout." The similarity of the criticism by famous eighteenth-, nineteenth-, and twentieth-century critics is striking in this respect:

> It is acknowledged with universal conviction, that the perusal of [Congreve's] works will make no man better; and that their ultimate effect is to represent pleasure in alliance with vice, and to relax those obligations by which life ought to be regulated. (Johnson)[2]

> What is immoral shall not be presented to the imagination of the young and susceptible in constant connexion with what is attractive. . . . And if it be asked why that age encouraged immorality which no other age would have tolerated, we have no hesitation in answering that this great depravation of the national taste was the

effect of the prevalence of Puritanism under the Commonwealth. (Macaulay)[3]

The theatre gave its sanction to [the manners of its audience]. By representing nothing but vice, it authorised their vices. Authors laid it down as a rule, that all women were impudent hussies, and that all men were brutes. Debauchery in their hands became a matter of course, nay more, a matter of good taste; they teach it. Rochester and Charles II could quit the theatre edified in their hearts; more convinced than ever that virtue was only a pretence, the pretence of clever rascals who wanted to sell themselves dear. (Taine)[4]

The courtiers made of the theatre a meeting-place of their own, with license of all kinds, bringing there their dubious loves, so that those citizens who still retained some of their Puritan convictions shunned the place like a plague. . . . In the comedies, and the comedies are but a reflex of real life, the citizens' wives are made fair game for the debauched sparks, their husbands the mere butts for ill-placed wit and buffoonery. . . . The spectators, then, for whom the poets wrote and the actors played were the courtiers and their satellites. The noblemen in the pit and boxes, the fops and beaux and wits or would-be-wits who hung on to their society, the women of the court, depraved and licentious as the men, the courtesans with whom these women of quality moved and conversed as on equal terms, made up at least four-fifths of the entire audience. Add a sprinkling of footmen in the upper gallery, a stray country cousin or two scattered throughout the theatre, and the picture of the audience is complete. (Nicoll)[5]

The atmosphere of the plays corresponded very closely with the atmosphere of a portion of society, . . . [comic] heroes were drawn from the characters of such persons as Sedley, Rochester, and Charles himself, and . . . however shocking the incidents and speeches might be, they are to be matched in dissoluteness by what is to be found in the histories and memoirs. . . . The dramatists cynically admire nothing but success, and satirize nothing but failure—failure to be graceful, failure to be witty, and failure in *savoir faire,* but not failure to be virtuous. (Krutch)[6]

What Restoration comedy does reveal, more than any other source, is the extent to which people were unbalanced; like Dada, for instance, it was the fever-chart of a sick society, a society that might easily have

The Attacks on Restoration Comedy

died. . . . I say "immoral" because this comedy is one of the symptoms of a sick society, and one of the things that society was sick of, naturally, was too much morality. (Wain)[7]

This catalogue could be amplified tenfold by including the critical observations of the *Spectator,* Thackeray, Meredith, Beljame, and others. But after reading several of these passages, one recalls that old cliché about reading Restoration comedies—they all begin to sound alike. The moral argument against Restoration comedy from Jeremy Collier to John Wain is based on these assumptions about the comedy and its society: from 1660 to 1698 the comic drama was written by, for, and about the unbridled libertines who galloped with Old Rowley. English society had been sexually and politically repressed during the Commonwealth period, so when Charles regained the throne, the whole society (but especially the upper class) lost its moral inhibitions and abandoned the social restraints endorsed and enforced by sober Puritans. The libertine holiday appeared to last for thirty-eight years. The audiences of these comedies narcissistically fawned upon their own images reflected most afternoons of the week at the Theatre Royal or the Duke's Theatre. (In the eighteenth-century Drury Lane Theatre, a large sign over the stage read *Veluti in speculum*—"Behold as in a glass.") The comedies not only reflected accurately the mores of a morally bankrupt coterie; they endorsed them. No plays with a traditional (or Christian) bias could survive on the stage, for the rakish lords and raffish orange girls would halt their groping in the pit or gallery just long enough to bury the playwright and cast with rotten vegetables and choruses of catcalls. The comic drama, after all, was written by, for, and about libertines. Anthony Hamilton's *The Memoirs of Count Grammont* and Pepys's *Diary* are presumptive evidence of a "sick" culture; the plays themselves confirm the diagnosis which many distinguished critics have agreed upon.

The conflation of drama and society into a single nauseating phenomenon is a central ploy in the attack on Restoration comedy. The equation of the comedy and its culture enables such literary historians as Taine, Beljame, Macaulay, and, to a lesser extent, Allardyce Nicoll to attack simultaneously the image which they create of the comic drama and its contemporary society. Macaulay's *History of England* (1848–61), for example, is in some ways an apologia for the author's age, a kind of Victorian *Aeneid*, and his biases are as much political as moral. Not one of his critics has ever accused him either of being objective or of forthrightly acknowledging the prejudices which inform his numerous moral and political judgments. In surveying England before the accession of James II, Macaulay suggests that the society was racked by the internecine battle between libertines and Whigs. His recital of the "shocking" episodes in Restoration social history is familiar to all students of the period—that is, to whoever reads the literary histories which enshrine the "received opinions." The arch-Whig Macaulay dilates indignantly on the turpitude of Charles II but just a few pages later dismisses as frivolous and insignificant the peccadilloes of good King William. The squalor of Charles's court, Macaulay maintains, shaped the moral code which society and the drama mimed. Restoration literature thus becomes little more than a social document—a fever-chart, to use Wain's metaphor, and one which gives an unfailing image of social reality. When one has read, say, several Restoration comedies, one "knows" the Restoration; or if one reads other social documents, one "knows" the plays.

This circular line of criticism reaffirms Collier's main points about the comedies' "profaneness and immorality" and echoes his moral fervor. Not until 1937 did an essay in *Scrutiny* change the tenor of the attack. L. C. Knights's famous essay, "Restoration Comedy: The Reality and the Myth" follows the *Scrutiny* formula par excellence: in a graceful and forceful manner, Knights radically devalues literature (in this case, Restoration drama) whose reputation either was well established or whose esteem had been elevated by recent studies. Knights abandons the Collier line, for morals are relevant "only in the long run"[8] and Knights, one presumes, does not intend to run very far. Of more immediate concern to him is the purely aesthetic interest of the plays, and on this count Knights finds the plays sorely

The Attacks on Restoration Comedy

deficient. "The criticism that defenders of Restoration comedy need to answer is not that the comedies are 'immoral', but that they are trivial, gross and dull" (p. 19). The comedies are trivial because their authors "bring to bear a miserably limited set of attitudes" (p. 9) on a miserably limited number of themes. They are gross not because sexual themes are so abundant but because the plays evince a sterile and platitudinous interest in sex: the dominant conventions are that "constancy in love, especially in marriage, is a bore"; appetite "needs perpetually fresh stimulation"; and the chase is all (pp. 12, 13). The Restoration audience demanded only that comedies be titillating, and however satisfactory the plays seemed to their cretinous audiences, Knights finds them a bore.

Knights relegates the moral issue to a minor position without ever dealing with it directly while ostensibly employing what he calls a "free and critical approach" (p. 4). He attacks the plays for mindlessly presenting parochial manners and ephemeral values. The so-called sparkling wit of the raillery is flatly banal because it fails to reflect "the best thought of the time" in "the speech of the people" (p. 4) as he considers the Elizabethan dramatists to have done. (He seems to restate Eliot's famous diagnosis of the "dissociation of sensibility," the besetting malaise of late seventeenth-century literature.) Whatever the limitations of this essay—it has been defended as well as attacked—it attempted by sleight-of-hand to conjure away the moral issue and concentrate evaluative criticism exclusively on aesthetic criteria, even though Knights indicates no awareness of the complexities which logically attend such a shift of emphasis. In any case Restoration comedy was found as deficient by Knights's new standards as by the old ones established by Collier.

Following Knights's arguments rather closely though not acknowledging Knights's essay, Arnold Kaul perceives the failure of Restoration comedy not as "its immorality but rather its lack of dramatic quality."[9] In a long chapter on the "inverted abstractions of Restoration comedy," Kaul contends that "the bulk of Restoration comedy involves little beyond a flat exemplification of a value system of remarkably uncomplicated and unexamined assumptions. No values or attitudes can be said to emerge from it since the condition for such emergence—the condition of enquiry, of conflict, of dramatic testing and endorsement—forms no part of its design" (p. 90). Just as Knights had observed that in Restoration comedy the fools are distinguishable from the heroes only "by the discrepancy between their ambitions and achievement, not because their ambitions are puerile" (p. 11), Kaul maintains that "however much the manner might differ superficially, the purposes and the pursuits [of hero and fool] are identical" (p. 94). The characters seem curiously monotonous because "the pleasure that everyone seeks in Restoration comedy is above all the pleasure of competition, of besting everyone else in the field" (p. 94). The famous "wit" is frequently only a vacuous mode of verbal competition. After all, anyone can invert moral commonplaces and create a "shocking" moral posture. "All pleasure is sinful: the only sin is to miss pleasure; love is a spiritual relationship: love is a carnal activity; love is deathless: love dies its natural death at the very moment of its satisfaction; marriage is an accepted bond of mutual esteem and fidelity: marriage is the recognized certificate of mutual distaste and infidelity; and so on" (p. 108). The absence of abstract intellectual conflict vitiates the drama. Even if the comedy is not gross (Kaul doesn't say that it is), it certainly is trivial and, with very few exceptions, dull. Without the interaction of dramatic perspectives, readers like Kaul lose interest. Though he briefly but favorably cites Thomas Fujimura's *The Restoration Comedy of Wit*, Kaul seems to concur with Knights that the plays are an intellectual desert, barren alike of "significant" ideas (Fujimura's book interprets the comedies in light of significant seventeenth-century intellectual traditions) and the multiple systems of value which he deems essential for first-rate comedy.

Kaul's essay, which introduces a new attack on Restoration comedy, ignores completely the moral dimension which had concerned critics for nearly three centuries. The moralist's objections have been quietly swept aside, supplanted by criteria of style and intellectual vitality.[10] These modern critics, to be sure, find Restoration comedy deficient but not because they expect

The Attacks on Restoration Comedy

drama to instruct or because Restoration comedy fails to be instructive or instructs perniciously. It is necessary only that comedy be entertaining, and the comedies fail here, too, perhaps because they reward "vitious persons" so predictably that dramatic tension and intellectual vitality disappear. Oscar Wilde's dictum—"There is no such thing as a moral or an immoral book. Books are well written, or badly written. That is all"—lingers like a specter over Knights's and Kaul's essays. Whether the spirit of Jeremy Collier has followed with interest the fortunes of the critical attack he began is a question I shall not presume to answer, but undoubtedly he would be pleased to see the comedies still under assault. He would be astounded, however, that his moral touchstone, for two centuries a cardinal issue in critical discussions of Restoration literature, is so blithely ignored by modern critics. A tradition which began with Collier ends, in a sense, with Oscar Wilde's epitaph, suggesting that criticism, like politics, sometimes makes for strange bedfellows.

2

"The Usefulness of the Stage": Restoration Comedy *Moralisé* and the *Réaliste* Tradition

Even though modern assailants of Restoration comedy have abandoned the moral axis, its defenders—from John Dennis to Virginia Ogden Birdsall—have persistently seen a moral value in the comedies they champion, though they have employed widely different criteria for determining how literature is moral and have devised different critical strategies to defend their positions. M. Pierre Legouis characterizes the problem in an amusing way. "Une amusante statistique établit que sur dix critiques écrivant entre 1915 et 1950, six la trouvent réaliste et sur ces six, deux la trouvent morale, deux immorale et deux amorale. Parmi les quatre critiques qui la trouvent artificielle deux la trouvent amorale et deux la condamnent comme immorale en dépit de son irréalité."[1] My examination of the *moralisé* tradition will consider the premises of the *réaliste* and *artificielle* criticism of Restoration comedy, since the latitude of those divisions allows for more precise discriminations later. What will be clearly shown is that a defense on moral grounds, regardless of the critic's acknowledged fondness for or aversion to explicitly ethical evaluations of literature, figures into much of the favorable criticism of Restoration comedy, both ancient and modern.

The usual distinction between the *réaliste* and *artificielle* schools depends on the critic's judgment that the comedies reflect a society which actually existed or that the "society" of Restoration

The *Réaliste* Tradition

comedy is a rarefied extrapolation from contemporary society, an aesthetic construction which has no exact correspondence in social history. I would like to retain that distinction but add this further one: the *réaliste* critics argue that the comedies achieve a moral effect because of the ethical content of the plays; the *artificielle* critics maintain that the comedies "free" the reader or spectator from pedestrian concerns and thus achieve their moral effect. If the plays have any significant intellectual or ethical content, that value would, at best, be incidental and ancillary if not wholly irrelevant.

Among the *réaliste* critics are three groups, each defined by a particular approach to the morality of Restoration comedy and each basing its arguments on "historical" evidence. The school assumes that the plays reflect accurately the social conditions of a coterie and thereby confirm the evidence afforded by nonliterary documents whose validity they do not question.

Regarding the plays as "realistic," these critics have found three ways to moralize the comedies. Some have seen in the comedies a serious "new philosophy," an amalgamation of Hobbes, Machiavelli, and French libertine wit. This "new philosophy" is regarded as a significant effort to adjust to cataclysmic cultural change—a king was beheaded, the Commonwealth failed, and the new king returned from France to the throne. Such changes demanded a new code of morality by which people could make sense of existence, and Restoration comedy is the most artful expression not only of the *Zeitgeist* but of the "new philosophy" as well. This seventeenth-century version of "future shock" produced a moral code—and this, I think, is the key point for many modern critics—that is very congenial with "the modern sensibility" (that is, the critics' own sense of life). This correspondence of values "proves" that the plays are moral, for the plays show characters attempting to survive in a world much like the modern world. Wycherley's Horner and Heller's Yossarian are against the same "system."

A second group among the *réalistes* would argue that within the plays is a coherent system of morality, one which later critics should not presume to judge. To describe the moral code affirmed by the plays is sufficient; to judge it either as moral or immoral is presumptuous and arrogant.

Finally, a third group sees the plays not only as "realistic" but as a repudiation of the "new philosophy" that the critics in the first category not only perceived but championed. These critics argue that the comedies affirm the moral values of Christian orthodoxy, not of the "new philosophy." When properly read, they argue, the comedies are as orthodox and edifying as most pieces of traditional apologetics. The Restoration dramatists provide a comic redaction of Christian morality.

To say that the critics in the first category find Restoration comedy moral is not to suggest either that their critical standards are necessarily debased or that they start each day's work by murmuring with Milton's Satan, "Evil be thou my good." Their discourse is never couched so baldly. But when they write about the beneficial moral effects of reading Restoration comedy, their critical strategies sometimes seem like the special pleading of medieval and Renaissance exegetes who sought and therefore found Christian truths in pagan writings by consciously moralizing the writings.[2] Like the exegetes of old, some critics of the comedies find the drama "moral" because (the logic is theirs, not mine) the plays seem "modern," which means, I take it, that the plays reflect their own sensibility. "There is real intellectual substance in these plays and indeed . . . that substance comes surprisingly close to our twentieth-century world-view,"[3] says Norman Holland. And in his conclusion to *The Restoration Comedy of Wit* Thomas Fujimura makes his conception of the "moral life" even more explicit than Holland's. The Restoration dramatists

> accepted the naturalness, and hence the rightness, of man's egoistic, hedonic, and malicious character. In accordance with this bias, Etherege and Wycherley, and to a lesser extent Congreve, depicted the characters in the plays as egoistic and libertine creatures interested in pleasure, both intellectual and sensual. . . . They indulged in witty criticism of conventional morality, arranged marriages, cant about honor, the pious pretenses of the clergy, and the folly of pretenders

The *Réaliste* Tradition

who went against nature. This insistence on naturalness, sincerity, and sound sense, and the exposure of all that goes contrary to these, is quite compatible with modern notions of morality.[4]

Though elsewhere in his book Fujimura becomes nearly as ethereal as Lamb,[5] he does provide a sound explanation of the seventeenth-century meanings of "wit." Such critics as Fujimura and Holland rely on a circular and dubious argument that Restoration comedy is moral because it seems modern. Just as Jan Kott finds Shakespeare his Polish contemporary, numerous critics have found their noble kinsmen in the works of Restoration playwrights. Their assumptions about art and morality demand further clarification.

First of all, the critics in this category reject Collier's conception of comedy and replace it with various theories about the psychoanalytic function of art. Similarly, they deride orthodox Christian assumptions about human nature and decorum, even though these assumptions were held by the vast majority in Restoration society. Although these critics frequently use historical sources to interpret the plays, their primary approach is ahistorical and psychoanalytical: Restoration comedy is peculiarly modern—that is, modern in a way that *Paradise Lost* or *Religio Laici* is not—because it symbolically enacts the concerns and anticipates (the exegetes of old would have referred to "type" and "antitype") the attitudes of such contemporaries as Freud and Norman O. Brown, both of whom emphasize the individual's struggle to achieve selfhood in an oppressive society. Freud, for example, finds that in his research into neurosis, he is led

> to make two reproaches against the super-ego of the individual. In the severity of its commands and prohibitions it troubles itself too little about the happiness of the ego, in that it takes insufficient account of the resistances against obeying them—of the instinctual strength of the id . . . and of the difficulties presented by the real external environment. . . . Consequently we are very often obliged, for therapeutic purposes, to oppose the super-ego, and we endeavour to lower its demands. Exactly the same objections can be made against the ethical demands of the cultural super-ego.[6]

CRITICS, VALUES, AND RESTORATION COMEDY

In a truly free and supportive society, the individual need no longer contend with the trammels of stifling conventions and taboos. A new order should arise, like the phoenix, from the ashes of the old moral order and harmoniously integrate the sexual instinct with the whole of man's interests and aspirations. The war against repression is a central theme in Brown's "modern" version of *Pilgrim's Progress,* wherein the world, the flesh, and the Devil are man's allies, not antagonists.

> The abolition of repression would abolish the unnatural concentrations of libido in certain particular body organs—concentrations engineered by the negativity of the morbid death instinct, and constituting the bodily base of the neurotic character disorders in the human ego. In the words of Thoreau: "We need pray for no higher heaven than the pure senses can furnish, a purely sensuous life. Our present senses are but rudiments of what they are destined to become." The human body would become polymorphously perverse, delighting in that full life of all the body which it now fears. The consciousness strong enough to endure full life would be no longer Apollonian but Dionysian—consciousness which does not observe the limit, but overflows; consciousness which *does not negate any more*.[7]

The function of art in this scheme of values is to dramatize the struggle of the individual toward freedom—toward life rather than toward death[8]—and thus provide a paradigm for the audience, whose members are presumably frustrated by the oppressive demands of traditional morality. Restoration comedy is moral ("therapeutic" is a common and telling synonym) because it provides a template of the universal struggle toward freedom.

An understanding of the modern sensibility, or at least its secular humanist strain, is essential for a full understanding of the assumptions which numerous critics regard as self-evident truths, and the writings of Freud and Brown roughly delineate the intellectual context of much modern criticism. These writings also enable one to comprehend more quickly G. Wilson Knight's ipse dixit about comedy in *The Golden Labyrinth:* "The proper function of comedy," he says magisterially, "is to assist the assimilation of instincts, especially sexual instincts."[9] And one

The *Réaliste* Tradition

can understand why Fujimura regards Freud's *Wit and Its Relation to the Unconscious* as a restatement of Aristotle's *Tractatus coislinianus* and then argues that "wit" comedy provides a purgative experience both moral and salubrious. "There is pleasure in skeptical, malicious, and sexual wit because our repressed tendencies are satisfied by the short cut provided by wit; and such relief from restraint is conducive to mental health. According to this theory, the vicarious satisfaction of our sexual, malicious, and cynical tendencies through wit comedy will make us less likely to express these tendencies directly, and perhaps dangerously, among our fellow men" (p. 64). And C. D. Cecil, in an article which begins as a study of raillery in Restoration comedy, soars to a grand peroration. "To read these comedies now and again in terms of Restoration concepts of verbal decorum should help us to comprehend better their theatrical efficacy.... The energy and the vitality of the characters matter enormously, for—as in Shaw—the brightest of them, however heterodox, are working for that ultimate harmony which one man can idealize as the peace of the Augustans and which another must project as far as human thought can reach."[10] Though Cecil acknowledges that the "morality matters as little as the morality of Jack Tanner's *Revolutionist's Handbook*," he seems so entranced by the vitality of the raillery that he envisions a new social order generated by verbal vitality alone.

Norman Holland, probably the most influential critic in this first category, defends the plays' morality on two grounds. Arguing that the major theme in Restoration comedy is the schism between "appearance" and "nature," he shows how "the conflict between 'manners' (i.e., social conventions) and anti-social 'natural' desires" (p. 4) interanimates eleven comedies by Etherege, Wycherley, and Congreve. He discusses the morality of the plays both directly and indirectly: in numerous passages he notes the "modernity" of the plays (besides the title of his book, see pp. 5, 8, 58, 62–63, 210, et passim). By showing their modernity, he implicitly argues the plays are moral. After all, the comedies share what he sees as a modern prepossession with freedom, development of one's self in a repressive society, the holistic harmonizing of one's sexual appetites, and so on. When more explicit, Holland attempts to explain how the plays are moral.

> The purpose of literature is to me simply pleasure, the pleasure of understanding, first the coherence and structure of the work itself and, second, the relation of the work to the reality it represents. The first kind of understanding involves such things as contrast, parallelism, images, or symbols; the second deals with life likeness, "character," probability, motivation, and the like. In both cases, "understanding" involves apprehending through a total activity of mind, emotions as well as discursive intelligence. If a play is true to its purpose, the pleasure of understanding, then I think it cannot be called immoral. (P. 3)

In the last chapter of his study, he is more succinct: "the plays have real intellectual substance and meaning; since they do, they are not immoral either, for they are true to the purpose of literature, 'the pleasure of understanding'" (p. 221). Holland's discovery of intellectual substance echoes the remarks of G. Wilson Knight, Fujimura, Freud, and Brown cited above. The aesthetic concern with style, separated from the moral concern by L. C. Knights and others, is once more fused in Holland's criticism. A well written work, it seems, can never be immoral because a well written work can be "understood" and thus is true to the purpose of literature; an obscure or incomprehensible work, I presume, could be "immoral" by Holland's criteria rather than merely unclear.

The argument is twofold. The comedies have a "moral" form (that is, they are intelligible) and a "moral" content because their concerns come "surprisingly close to *our* [my italics] twentieth-century world-view" (p. 8). It is doubtful, of course, whether "our" includes such modern critics as T. S. Eliot, C. S. Lewis, and Yvor Winters, for example. To be more precise, the morality he finds congenial is but one kind of morality in modern society. Just as Jeremy Collier had assumed a consensus about what his contemporaries valued and believed when he attacked the plays

The *Réaliste* Tradition

on their behalf, Holland becomes the *soi-disant* spokesman for modern morality as he champions the plays.

Virginia Ogden Birdsall's *Wild Civility: The English Comic Spirit on the Restoration Stage* (1970), a lengthy study of eleven plays, is indebted to Holland's study as well as to Johan Huizinga's *Homo Ludens* and such contemporary writers as Havelock Ellis, Freud, and Susanne Langer. The passages from Freud and Brown as well as Holland's criticism provide the proper context for understanding her work, especially her use of "moral" and "natural."

> Horner is (and in part by virtue of his very "wickedness") a wholly positive and creative comic hero, and . . . much of the imagery of the play places him squarely on the side of health, of freedom, and most controversial of all, of honesty.[11]

> The Restoration comic hero does not turn the world of inherited rules upside down merely for the smutty or destructive fun of it. If he is self-consciously wicked, it is because the prevailing system has proved repressive of his *élan vital* and hence prompts him to demand more flexible and expressive forms. For him the only true morality is living well and fully. (P. 20)

> [The comic hero, like Vice figure] is "devilish" in a positive, life-assertive sense, and he reveals through his character and actions the constructive possibilities of at least some of the human vices. His sphere of action is, significantly, the same as that of his negative counterpart, for more often than not he too attacks "family unity and love." . . . But he does so only when they have abandoned their creative potential, when they have proved to be repressive of vitality or have become mere words and forms, empty of any genuinely constructive promise, and hence no longer sources of life but deadening restrictions. (P. 30)

Birdsall considers the rake-hero as "player," following Huizinga closely in describing the seriousness of "play" in art and culture, as "libertine," and as a "Vice" figure. Synthesizing these three roles in her perception of the rake-hero, she sees characters like Horner achieve "that ideal which has been ascribed to the humanistic Greeks: 'the happy union of natural exuberance with a sense of style which does not impede but gives it a direction and a distinction'" (p. 39). To put it another way, Birdsall follows the "party line" in regard to the morality of the comedies, for she sees in them a struggle between two forces as easily identifiable as the heroes and villains in any melodrama: on one hand there is the unrestrained, exuberant, antitraditional, life-affirming rake-hero; on the other is the inflexible, dogmatic, repressive, life-denying society which must be "gleefully and triumphantly challenged by the defiant individual" (p. 4). If there are hierarchies of characters within the comedies or if there are gradations and mixtures of vices and virtues, she does not mention them. Her key assumptions, critical and moral, lock her into a dualism as rigid as Collier's.

Like the other critics in this group, Birdsall views the comedies as moral because she sees one kind of modern sensibility in the plays. In this light the comedies become comic precursors of *Prometheus Unbound*, whose eponymous hero is instrumental in inaugurating a reign of love, natural, spontaneous, and unrepressed; their morality derives from the moral appropriateness of struggling for liberation against an ossified social order. The attitude toward sexuality, a particular concern of the opponents of the plays, is celebrated as "healthy," "free," and "open" even though, as Arnold Kaul astutely points out, "Restoration comedy carefully designates women as whores, mistresses, or wives, [characteristically treating] all without distinction as commodities—some to be paid for by one party and some by another, but none acceptable or available without a price" (p. 96).

Whereas Fujimura, Holland, Birdsall, and others offer many incisive observations about particular comedies, their general approach to the plays suggests an unconscious projection of several modern prejudices onto the comedies, and their theories require them to distort considerably some plays (Birdsall's remarks on Horner, for example) in order to support their thesis. Their strategy in the *moralisé* tradition is not to praise folly but to explain folly to the reader in such a way that folly becomes virtue in masquerade. When the vizard-mask is ripped off, the plays are both modern and moral.

The *Réaliste* Tradition

If the first group of *réaliste* critics makes modernity the Siamese twin of morality, the second group pleads that what seems to us shocking behavior is in fact "moral" behavior when judged by contemporary (i.e., Restoration) standards. These critics see the characters as an accurate reflection of Restoration social types whose code of ethics, like the code of every age, represents its own kind of morality and should not be judged by later ages. The characters' "immorality and profaneness" are attenuated, if not eliminated, when one becomes familiar with the social codes which supplanted the austere Puritan regime. Jean Gagen, for example, maintains that in Mirabell, the rake-hero of *The Way of the World*, "the late seventeenth-century ideal of the gentleman, with both its shortcomings and its peculiar virtues, is mirrored with remarkable fidelity."[12] Using several contemporary conduct books, Gagen suggests that "Mirabell has behaved in accordance with the ideals of the gentleman as they were then understood" (p. 427). (One might recall Dr. Johnson's comment on the most famous of the conduct books of the eighteenth century, Chesterfield's *Letters to His Son:* the volume teaches "the manners of a dancing-master and the morals of a whore." Johnson was not notably sympathetic to relativism in matters of morality.) In a similar vein D. R. M. Wilkinson uses the concept of decorum in contemporary courtesy literature to study the comedies; he finds that the characters were in no way immoral by the standards of the beau monde. On the contrary, they embody the ideals of the social code by which he believes the audience lived.[13] Continuing in this tradition, David S. Berkeley argues that the putative sexual license is not erotic if one is familiar with the social and literary conventions of *préciosité*. "The Restoration comedy of manners is an aristocratic reaction against an aristocratic vogue; and one may suppose that the license of manners comedy is extreme, judged by English standards, because of the lofty pretensions and ridiculous formalities of its other half, *précieuse* gallantry."[14] The comedies, far from being immoral, corrected the extravagant manners of an alien social code. The naturalistic candor of the anti-*précieuse* elements must be seen as the dramatists' attempt to extirpate offensive French mannerisms. The "morality" of the playwrights' enterprise is irreproachable, according to Berkeley's thesis, though such moralists as Milton or Bunyan might ponder whether the remedy was not worse than the disease.

While one group finds the manners satirized, another group of critics regards the manners of the beau monde as exemplary models of conduct endorsed by their culture. Within the scope of this essay it is not possible to settle this question, though it clearly bears upon the moral vision of these comedies. Of more immediate interest are three articles which deal directly with the problem of sexual morality in Restoration comedy. In 1929 Guy Montgomery questioned "whether there were not beneath those *manners,* a system of ideas, of which the manners, and incidentally, the comedy, were not a 'realization.'"[15] Answering his own question, he concludes that the empiricism of the Royal Society partially explains the new moral code. An atmosphere in which "old truths" and social customs were scrutinized as closely, say, as the circulatory system of mongrels is a symbol of the pervasive spirit of the Royal Society. The new way of the world, to paraphrase the motto of the Royal Society, is to take the word of no man—in science or in conduct. Thus Montgomery cannot "help detecting in the over-boldness of men and women in their relationships and in the frankness of their conduct, instead of an abandonment of all moral standards, an approach to conduct, if not technically scientific, yet genuinely experimental" (p. 35).

The challenge that the witty couples made to orthodox courtship customs is, for Montgomery, a splendid civic contribution. "It is questionable, however, whether a social order will survive if it does not from time to time subject its foundations to a search for weak spots. It is probably a fact that an honest social order never was; there have been times when society was in the process of *becoming* honest. Thanks to *Restoration* comedy, I think we have preserved for us a fairly faithful picture of a society at one of these 'becoming' times" (pp. 36–37). Since the greatest challenge to conventional social values and conduct is in the area of sexual relations, the frankness of the men and women is an exuberant "reaffirmation of the individual's inalienable privilege to

The *Réaliste* Tradition

live naturally in a world whose limits were rapidly becoming circumscribed, on the one hand by a popular conventional moral code, and on the other was being extended by scientific and social experiment and research as they had not been extended by the discoveries of the sixteenth century" (p. 40). For Montgomery, Restoration comedy challenges the critic to perceive and sympathize with the moral code embodied by the plays, for in the inevitable pattern of keeping, courting, and cuckolding, certain inalienable rights are symbolically affirmed.

No less hortatory but somewhat more historical is P. F. Vernon's "Marriage of Convenience and the Moral Code of Restoration Comedy," an article which supports and documents in more detail several of Montgomery's assertions about Restoration marriage contracts. Vernon contends that a study of marital conventions in Restoration comedy reveals "a wholly consistent moral standpoint," a moral stance in stark rebellion against the contemporary view of marriage as an opportunity to consolidate the estates of landed families. After studying the mercenary union of economics and marriage, Vernon thus describes the nature of sexual relations in the comedies:

> Many of those comedies which take delight in a triumphant cuckolding are making an indirect comment on an important social theme. Defiant adultery proclaims the cause of free-choice in sexual relationships against a despised financial institution. The mercenary, old husband has been outwitted, the young lovers lie in one another's arms, and the audience shares in a gesture of contempt at the claims to sanctity of contemporary marriage and at the whole duty of man. There need be no sympathy for the cuckold; he deserves his fate. . . . Men who identified themselves so shamelessly with the mercenary system had only themselves to blame if their wives respected neither husbands nor the marriage-vows which had been forced from them.[16]

Vernon sees the persistent cuckolding themes as a comment on iniquitous social and economic practices; marriage is at the center of corruption and thus is to be challenged as an affirmation of free moral choice.

Considering the moral value of the comedies in a slightly different context, F. W. Bateson regards the sexual jokes as having a serious social function. "If the political problem *par excellence* in the second half of the seventeenth century was to avoid the recurrence of a second Civil War, its social parallel, essentially, was to rationalize the sex instinct. Until such a rationalization had been achieved genuine communication between Whigs and Tories was hardly possible. Intermarriage, the final solution, was unthinkable. . . . From one point of view, in the mode of allegory proper to high comedy, the Restoration drama records the strains that accompanied the achievement."[17] Bateson argues that the comedies were instrumental in socially uniting the conflicting factions. Implicit is his belief not only in the existence but the efficacy of the "mode of allegory proper to high comedy," a mode which makes the "ultimate 'meaning' of *The Country Wife* a statement about politics: Horner, 'the sophisticated Man of Sense' . . . emerges as a Grotesque or mere mechanism, and Margery, the primitive country girl, stands for the ordinary human decencies. The Tories were, of course, the Country Party" (p. 31). This *post hoc ergo propter hoc* argument maintains that the comedies were morally efficacious, for another Civil War did not occur, and a cohesive society did emerge in the next century. Bateson's use of the "allegorical mode" to disclose "ultimate meaning" in *The Country Wife* places him squarely in the *moralisé* tradition. The medieval and Renaissance exegetes, proud of their hermeneutical skills, would be pleased to find such a distinguished modern critic returning to their spirit and method of reading profane literature.

About the critics in this second section one can observe several distinguishing traits. All argue that the comedies are moral, but they perceive the morality as the unique creation of seventeenth-century philosophers and playwrights. The moral code of the plays can be understood, they maintain, only by examining the nexus between contemporary social problems and the expression of those problems in drama. The comedies express a high standard of morality because they identify social ills (the miseries of enforced marriage or the cloying artificiality of the *précieuse* conventions) or reflect the most genteel standards of conduct

The *Réaliste* Tradition

available to society or have a high comic seriousness which mollified potentially explosive political factions. Unlike the critics in the first category, these critics do not argue that the Weltanschauung of Restoration comedy particularly suits modern needs or reflects distinctly modern values. Instead they show that the ethos of the drama reflects a type of morality completely appropriate to that society. The usual moral objections to Restoration comedy, they would say, are the product of rigid moral absolutism, ignorance of social conditions during the Restoration, misconceptions about the ways in which comedies are morally useful, or a combination of these deficiencies. Making the distinction another way, one might say that Jeremy Collier and his ilk might regard contemptuously the infamous activities of Barbara Villiers, countess of Castlemaine and mother of several illegitimate children by Charles II, and brand her as the Royal Whore; Norman Holland et alia might see her as a fully liberated woman, a champion of women's rights and arch-foe of the "double standard"; Bateson and his peers might soberly observe that her social activism was an appropriate response to the social problems of her day and her behavior was possibly sanctioned by the most fashionable conduct books of her age.

The third group of *réaliste* critics takes a different approach to the morality of the plays. This group argues that the comedies are moral, not because they appeal to or reflect a "modern" sensibility or because they were moral by radically new standards, but because they affirm traditional moral beliefs. Two of Collier's contemporary opponents, William Congreve and John Dennis, initiate this tradition. In his *Amendments of Mr. Collier's False and Imperfect Citations* (1698), Congreve is hard pressed to respond to all of Collier's points, so he first engages in *ad hominem* reflections on the clergyman's metaphors, motives, vanity, and ignorance.[18] Following Aristotle's definition of comedy as "an Imitation of the worst sort of people (*imitatio pejorum*)" (p. 7), Congreve justifies the presentation of "vitious" characters in the plays. "There are Crimes too daring and too horrid for Comedy. But the Vices most frequent, and which are the common Practice of the looser sort of livers, are subject Matter of comedy. . . . Men are to be laugh'd out of their Vices in Comedy; the Business of Comedy is to delight, as well as to instruct: And as vicious People are made asham'd of their Follies or Faults, by seeing them expos'd in a ridiculous manner, so are good People at once both warn'd and diverted at their Expence" (p. 8).

Congreve's defense grants Collier's premise that comedy is didactic and describes the manner in which it achieves its purpose, assuming, of course, that the follies and faults are presented so clearly and forcefully that the audience will readily discriminate between the vicious and the virtuous. Good people are at once "warn'd and diverted," says Congreve. (These sentiments are rather similar to Pepys's remarks about *L'Ecole des Filles,* which he bought with shame and read with haste for its moral instruction alone: it is "a mighty lewd book, but yet not amiss for a sober man once to read over to inform himself in the villainy of the world.") The crux of Congreve's argument is that the audience is led to repudiate, not imitate, the "common Practice of the looser sort of livers."

Sharing Congreve's assumptions about the drama, John Dennis defends the stage more systematically in *The Usefulness of the Stage* (1698) and in his *Defence of Sir Fopling Flutter* (1722). In the first work he offers a closely knit argument "that the Stage is more particularly Instrumental to the Happiness of Englishmen" because they suffer more seriously than other Europeans "from the reigning Distemper of the Clime, which is inseparable from the Spleen, from that gloomy and sullen Temper, which is generally spread through the Nation; from that natural Discontentedness, which makes us so uneasy to one another, because we are so uneasy to ourselves."[19] Only the drama can enable Englishmen to cope with their climatic malady. By catharsis (Dennis speaks primarily of tragedy in his first tract but his argument can be extended to include the effects of comedy) the passions are rendered more manageable. As for Collier's charge that the comedies corrupted the morals of Restoration society, Dennis asserts that the absence of public theatres during the Common-

The *Réaliste* Tradition

wealth was a more likely cause of Restoration excesses (I, p. 151).

But since plays moderate the passions of the audience and instruct men in their duty to God, their neighbors, and their king, the drama actually encourages the practice of Christianity. Collier's complaint that the nobility and clergy are slandered by the comic poets is rebutted by arguing that the characters should be perceived allegorically. "The Characters in every Comedy are always, at the bottom, universal and allegorical, or else the Instruction could not be universal. A ridiculous or vicious Priest in a Comedy, signifies any Man who has such Follies or Vices, and the Cassock is produc'd on purpose to signify to the Clergy, that they are partly concern'd in the Instruction, and have sometimes their Vices and Follies, as well as the Laity" (I, p. 187).

In his lengthy rebuttal of Collier's attack, Dennis develops three arguments: 1) drama is valuable to the state and to organized religion because it assists the citizens in regulating their passions and controlling their impulses; 2) it provides instruction and diversion; and 3) it exposes vices and follies to ridicule. His defense of *The Man of Mode* nearly twenty years later can be favorably compared to Dryden's celebrated critique of *The Silent Woman* in his *Essay of Dramatic Poesie:* both critics cogently apply their general critical principles in "practical criticism" of a famous comedy written about fifty years earlier.

The personal background of Dennis's *Defence* is germane only to the extent that he disagrees with Sir Richard Steele about the lineaments of a "fine Gentleman" in comedy. (Collier's ironic definition of the "fine Gentleman" is relevant to their quarrel, too.) In the *Spectator* and in his new play, *The Conscious Lovers*, Steele insists that the comic hero shall be honest at all times and refined in his language: these qualities are seldom found in the rake-heroes of Restoration comedy, so Steele supplants the "old" hero with a self-consciously virtuous young man. This conception of the comic hero, in Dennis's estimation, destroys comedy. "How little do they know of the Nature of true Comedy, who believe that its proper Business is to set us Patterns for Imitation: For all such Patterns are serious Things, and Laughter is the

Life, and the very Soul of Comedy. 'Tis its proper Business to expose Persons to our View, whose Views we may shun, and whose Follies we may despise; and by shewing us what is done upon the Comick Stage, to shew us what ought never to be done upon the Stage of the World."[20]

Dennis defends Dorimant, the object of Steele's scorn, on two grounds: his representation is decorous (i.e., he behaves appropriately for a young man of his station), and Dorimant is a judiciously selected representative of his age. As Horace is his authority for the first judgment, Rapin is his guide for the second. "Comedy is as it ought to be, when an Audience is apt to imagine, that instead of being in the Pit and Boxes, they are in some Assembly of the Neighbourhood, or in some Family Meeting, and that we see nothing done in it, but what is done in the World. For it is . . . not worth one Farthing, if we do not discover ourselves in it, and do not find in it both our own Manners, and those of the Persons with whom we live and converse" (II, p. 248). Dennis clearly recognizes Dorimant's moral flaws—his perfidy, lustfulness, vanity, and irascibility—but he regards them as traits wholly decorous for the negative *exemplum* Etherege created. By modeling the excesses of Dorimant and Sir Fopling Flutter after contemporary vices, Dennis argues, Etherege was able to achieve the highest aims of comedy: "to expose upon the Stage the Defects of particular Persons, in order to correct and amend the People, by the Fear of being laugh'd at" (p. 249).

Despite Pope's caricature of him as the ill-mannered critic, Dennis's arguments are still used by modern critics and in most cases are at least as lucid and insightful as those of his successors. Early in this century Dudley Miles proposed that Restoration comedy, using ironic inversions of moral commonplaces, reinforced traditional moral beliefs. Unlike John Dennis or Miles's contemporary, John Palmer, he assumes that the Restoration audience was "moral" (i.e., held traditional Christian attitudes and values); if the audience did not already have the proper moral predispositions, the "witty" inversions of traditional morality would be a witless parade of contemporary moral clichés. The players' remarks about sex are his case in point.

The *Réaliste* Tradition

> But is it not obvious that they never would have made such a topic subject for pleasantry if Restoration society had been so unconsciously corrupt as Mr. Palmer makes it out to have been? It was only because of their clear consciousness of the traditional belief that love and faithfulness accompany marriage that they uttered these witticisms. It was only because bourgeois standards were so perfectly familiar that the circle of Whitehall had an inexhaustible source of paradox. Otherwise much of the most brilliant dialogue in English comedy would have seemed to its first auditors little more than a series of platitudes.[21]

Miles's thesis rests on his assumptions about the audience: if the audience had the "right" values and saw in the plays a consistent pattern of verbal irony, then the comedies are moral. Whereas Dennis defended the plays for the acerbity of their social criticism, Miles praises the orthodoxy reinforced by their ironic wit. Thus he would have the reader believe that a contemporary audience would see the "traditional" morality in Sir John Brute's remarks, say, about marriage: "What cloying Meat is Love—when Matrimony's the Sauce to it! Two Years Marriage has debauch't my five Senses. Every thing I see, every thing I hear, every thing I feel, every thing I smell, and every thing I taste—methinks has Wife in it. . . . Sure there's a secret Curse entail'd upon the very Name of Wife" (I.i). Or in Sir Oliver Cockwood's: "To a true-bred gentleman all lawful solace is abomination."[22] Miles would argue that the ironic reversal of the beliefs held by the audience transforms these lines, even though they are uttered by fools in the plays—and to be fair to Miles, he does not quote these lines—into an analogue of the opening lines of the Anglican rite of marriage. Holy matrimony is

> an honourable estate, instituted of God in the time of man's innocency, signifying unto us the mystical union that is betwixt Christ and his Church: which holy estate Christ adorned and beautified . . . and therefore is not by any to be enterprised, nor taken in hand unadvisedly, lightly, or wantonly, to satisfy men's carnal lusts and appetites, like brute beasts that have no understanding; but reverently, discreetly, advisedly, soberly, and in the fear of God; duly considering

the causes for which Matrimony was ordained. (*The Book of Common Prayer*)

The playwrights' wit, when properly construed, is a means of traditional moral instruction. Irony is the alembic in which the base views of many characters are transmuted into sacramental gold.

Two more recent articles argue that the comedies provide traditional moral instruction either through a consistently satirical perspective or, in the case of Congreve's comedies, through a persistent regard for the demands of poetic justice. An investigation of seventeenth-century aesthetics by Charles O. McDonald convinces the author that Restoration comedy is "a fully adult form of satiric and comic art" written "by people who accepted ethical standards for their works of art."[23] McDonald grants more credence to the dramatists' claims about the didactic properties of their works than is usually granted because he sees the comedies as the culmination of three influences: "Ben Jonson and the humours tradition; non-dramatic materials of a classically-derived nature such as Theophrastan character sketches and Aristotlean and neo-Aristotlean rhetoric and psychology in Hobbes; and new developments in comic critical theory in Restoration England itself" (p. 523). Finding no "romantic" hero in the comedies, McDonald sees instead a moral hierarchy—he calls it "a satiric scale of ridicule" (p. 544)—in which all characters are ridiculed. The prologue to *The Provok'd Wife* suggests how McDonald approaches the plays.

> *Since 'tis the Intent and Business of the Stage,*
> *To Copy out the Follies of the Age;*
> *To hold to every Man a Faithful Glass,*
> *And shew him of what Species he's an Ass:*
> *I hope the next that teaches in the School*
> *Will shew our Author he's a scribbling Fool.*

The plays are designed to arouse in the audience a Hobbesian sense of superiority of which laughter is the natural expression. Like Puck, the audience is to perceive what fools those mortals be. McDonald admits that the comic dramatists may have been

The *Réaliste* Tradition

wrong "in expecting their audiences to respond with laughter to the whole of the carefully proportioned hierarchies of aberrant intelligence from fools to knaves exhibited in these plays, . . . hoping that the intelligence of their audiences (with a few notable exceptions like Dennis) was much greater than that of the characters" (pp. 542–43). But McDonald adduces historical evidence to indicate that the comedies offer not a right way/wrong way choice (Holland's thesis) but only a choice among subtly differentiated wrong ways. The audience was expected to recognize negative *exempla* and then repudiate the "wrong ways," discerning with unerring vision the kinds of aberrant intelligence represented in the dramatis personae. Opponents of this view might recall Pope's lines from *An Essay on Man:*

> *Vice is a monster of so frightful mien,*
> *As, to be hated, needs but to be seen;*
> *Yet seen too oft, familiar with her face,*
> *We first endure, then pity, then embrace.*
> *(II.217–20)*

When various degrees of evil are presented, the lesser evils are elevated to a position of relative superiority, if not transmogrified into "good" itself. McDonald's historical orientation is accurate, but his argument rests on the presumption of extraordinary percipience in the audience, at best a risky presumption since the comments of contemporary playgoers fail to show the sensitivity McDonald's thesis requires of them.

Creating a different historical milieu for Congreve's works, but arguing like the other critics in this group that the comedies enforce a traditional morality, Aubrey Williams insists that Congreve's corpus can be adequately understood only in light of the traditional Christian view of Providence. Since the works affirm the Christian view of Providence so common in contemporary apologetics, Williams contends that they "are fully conformable to the Christian vision of human experience which still prevailed at the end of the seventeenth century, that they are perhaps the wittiest of that same century's countless justifications of the ways of God to man, and that they were written, indeed, squarely in

CRITICS, VALUES, AND RESTORATION COMEDY

the face of those who would consign the universe to chance or mere necessity and who would consign all human events to fortune or appetite."[24]

This thesis strikes at the heart of Collier's objections to Restoration comedy, namely, its patent defiance of the demands of poetic justice. By showing the congruity of religious doctrine and literary technique, Williams argues for the morality of the plays. The first two-thirds of his essay develops an historical context that shows the critics and the theologians shared a common analogy: poetic justice mimes the Providential ordering of human affairs. Thus drama "could perform its supreme ethical function *only* by the closest possible imitation of a metaphysical reality—the reality of Providence" (p. 547). Williams maintains that Congreve guarantees for each character in every work the proper reward or punishment; his concern for a pattern of moral justice is "fully as 'providential' as it is 'poetical,'" (p. 565) and his works, therefore, are indubitably moral in design.

Williams argues learnedly and subtly, and his argument seems sound unless one actually considers, say, the thematic similarity of *The Old Batchelour* and *Paradise Lost*. Williams candidly confesses that he had no time to consider "the obvious dimensions of Congreve's work (i.e., matters of tone, style, and so on)" (p. 540), preferring to delay that discussion for another occasion. But those *obvious* matters, after all, are of considerable importance in shaping the meaning of a play. To be convincing, Williams's thesis must be rigorously applied to a criticism of individual comedies by Congreve and other dramatists. But like Miles and McDonald, he argues that a contemporary audience would have derived from Congreve's comedies traditional Christian wisdom: the comedies are not only an afternoon's diversion but are as instructive as the sermons of any Anglican divine.

Probably the most revolutionary approach to the morality of Restoration comedy is Ben Ross Schneider's *The Ethos of Restoration Comedy* (1971). Like Williams, Schneider argues that "the stage was clearly aware that it functioned as an alternative to the pulpit as a medium of instructing the populace."[25] After dismiss-

The *Réaliste* Tradition

ing other critics' remarks about "the extraliterary nature" of morality in these comedies, Schneider affirms that the plays have a decidedly moral content because they are satires, a type of art which necessarily implies both "an ethical aim and a method for achieving it" (p. 14). The audience sees a panorama of characters, "some to be shunned and some to be copied. [But which] is which?" (p. 16). Poetic justice provides the answer. The author recommends some moral traits by rewarding characters who possess them and discommends others by showing the ridiculous or humiliating consequences suffered by whoever has those traits. To discover the ethos of Restoration comedy is "only a matter of stating the characteristics of rewarded and punished characters" (p. 16). Schneider's approach is thus quite simple: he surveys 1,127 characters in eighty-three comedies and discovers their "ethical common denominators" by computing the frequency with which 113 different characteristics appear. Realizing that the computer has but a binary sensibility, Schneider only asks questions answerable affirmatively or negatively.

Schneider's first problem was dividing the characters—all 1,127 of them—into two groups, antagonists and protagonists. By his definition, a protagonist is "any character whose enterprises succeeded at the end of the play, whose behavior was praised by a reliable character, whose efforts were rewarded, or who . . . participated in the victory of the protagonists in some way or other" (p. 19). The antagonist, of course, is the opposite. Despite the clarity of this taxonomy, Schneider was unable to categorize 21 percent of the characters (there are 463 protagonists, 418 antagonists, and 246 who cannot be classified). But, he cautions, to recognize the virtues and vices of these characters, the critics must "overcome the cultural conditioning that causes us, like Collier, to read virtues as vices" and then "identify which characteristics of the great many attributed to a character qualify him for praise or blame" (p. 16). These caveats, couched in the language of scientific axioms, are particularly revealing, for they suggest a good deal about the moral orientation which controls the computer's conclusions. After all, if Schneider is to analyze the virtues and the vices, he must be confident of his own capacity and authority to distinguish between them: his criteria are relevant to his criticism, especially since he recognizes so clearly the limitations of Collier's moral vision. Unfortunately, Schneider is vague about his own "cultural conditioning" and does not even provide the 113-item profile on which he records the moral bias of the comedies and judges the moral properties of 1,127 characters. Such an omission is regrettable, for it might have been possible to discover the moral prejudices of the "judge" by examining the questions he asked and the answers which he found satisfactory.

Schneider explains that the five moral virtues central to Restoration comedy (generosity, liberality, courage, plain-dealing, and love) are a synthesis of the highest ethical principle in Plato's *Republic*, Aristotle's *Ethics*, the New Testament, Cicero's *De officiis*, and Castiglione's *The Courtier*, and he devotes a chapter to each virtue and its antagonistic vice. The greatest of these virtues is generosity, which epitomizes the ethos of Restoration comedy. "By rewarding generous actions, the comedies tell us what we ought to be.... By deflating moralistic, religious, and romantic pretensions they remind us that we are fallen humanity" (p. 182).

Prior to that conclusion, Schneider discloses that

> insofar as there is evidence, ... Restoration comedy approves of marrying for money only in cases of dire necessity. (P. 59)

> If a comic hero did happen to have a Christian faith, he could not decorously reveal it, especially in a world where protestations of religious faith were the province of zealots. (P. 108)

> The plays are more sympathetic toward common and kept women than they are toward any others engaged in commerce. Of the 37 whores, 13 are rewarded with settlements or husbands and 7 have no moral status at all, but are merely introduced to serve as comment on the moral status of other characters. On the others, the plays equivocate. Almost as many whores are rewarded as are held up to contempt, but on close inspection it appears that whoredom is not the cause of their being shamed: six of these eleven exhibit ill humor

The *Réaliste* Tradition

when they do not get their way, a breach of decorum which the plays always punish. (P. 111)

Schneider's method, in other words, is to approach the plays statistically; he tells us the odds of finding, say, a protagonist who sullies a lady's good name or an ill-humored whore no longer interested in commerce. But Schneider provides no readings of individual comedies and shows no awareness of the complexities that attend such an analysis. Nor does he draw any firm and unequivocal conclusions about the cumulative effect of having, for example, 63 percent "generous" protagonists and 37 percent "mean" antagonists on the comic stage. What, then, does he conclude about the ethos or morality of the comedies? He reduces the comedies to an archetypal pattern the orthodoxy of which even Jeremy Collier would applaud.

> The spectacle they present over and over again of weak woman humbling strong man, of softness overcoming hardness, of impetuous virility quenched by female calm, is a representation of the great joke about Mars and Venus that provoked the laughter of the gods. When a Careless Ramble or a Wildish is caught in the net of responsibility, baited with the very delicacy that he has so often consumed with impunity, what is there left to say about his many victories in the sex war? Man is a social animal. The family is his natural state. . . . While Restoration comedy prudently attends to the preservation of the species by making sure that mothers will be supported, that children will have fathers, and that estates will have heirs, it enjoys a huge laugh at the expense of the brave little fellows who thought that they could defy the law of kind. (Pp. 182–83)

An endorsement of connubial joy is the "meaning" of Restoration comedy, the final testament of the role of generosity in decently ordering human life on the stage and in real life. The cumulative effect of Restoration comedy when properly read, according to Schneider and the other *moralisé* critics in this section, is moral edification of the most conventional kind. Whereas Collier saw lewdness and Knights found boredom in the tedious emphasis on bedroom chatter, these *réaliste* critics see in the comedies a dramatic redaction of the morality of *The Book of*

Common Prayer or *Pilgrim's Progress*. Though their rhetorical tactics differ, the *moralisé* critics concur that the content and effect of Restoration comedy are moral. In the next chapter I examine how the *artificielle* critics, approaching the problem from quite different perspectives, arrive at the same conclusion.

3
"Escape from this dull age": The *Artificielle* Tradition

The assumptions and arguments of the *artificielle* critics are virtually the same from Lamb to the present group of critics who deplore Lamb's naïveté but who use both his central argument and sometimes even his rhetorical style. This group is not comprised exclusively of the "manners" critics, but it does include them. The distinctive feature of this group is its assumption about how comedies are moral: Restoration comedy is moral not because it is a faithful reflection of manners, though the "manners" critics emphasize this point, but because comedy grants the audience a respite from its mundane concerns and anxieties. The artifice of the spectacle—mistaken identities, staccato repartee, blinding flashes of wit, the silken gowns and scented gloves of the beau monde—all of these "anesthetize" the audience into an "artificial" experience of life. Such an escape has a salutary effect and thus an unarguable social value, so the plays are moral. These critics arrive at this final assessment from perspectives as different as nineteenth-century impressionistic criticism and modern historical criticism, but the fountainhead for the whole school is the criticism of Restoration comedy by Hazlitt and Lamb.

William Hazlitt's lecture on Wycherley, Congreve, Vanbrugh, and Farquhar (1819) is unusually generous to each of these writers. Having announced in an earlier lecture that he preferred Restoration comedy to Shakespearean, Hazlitt explains more fully in this lecture why he finds the comedies so satisfying. More than anything else, he admires the "style" of the comic writers, though it is difficult to tell whether he refers to the verbal gymnastics, the Baroque setting, the social games of the beau monde, or to the ambience created by all of these. Hazlitt's enthusiasm and lyrical language are a good introduction to the critics in this category.

> To read a good comedy is to keep the best company in the world, where the best things are said, and the most amusing happen. The wittiest remarks are always ready on the tongue, and the luckiest occasions are always at hand to give birth to the happiest conceptions. . . . We don't know which to admire most, the observation, or the answer to it. We would give our fingers to be able to talk so ourselves, or to hear others talk so. In turning over the pages of the best comedies, we are almost transported to another world, and escape from this dull age to one that was all life, and whim, and mirth, and humour. . . . Happy thoughtless age, when kings and nobles led purely ornamental lives; when the utmost stretch of a morning's study went no farther than the choice of a sword-knot, or the adjustment of a side-curl; when the soul spoke out in all the pleasing eloquence of dress; and beaux and belles, enamoured of themselves in one another's follies, fluttered like gilded butterflies, in giddy mazes, through the walks of St. James's Park![1]

Of primary importance are Hazlitt's emphasis on "escape" from the workaday world, his idealized conception of Restoration London, his admiration of verbal brilliance, and his admiration of Baroque manners ("the purely ornamental lives"). His commentary on individual playwrights is appreciative, not critical, and because his criticism was originally presented as lectures at the Surrey Institute, it relies more on extensive quotation from than analysis of the plays. If there is a moral or thematic dimension of the plays—if the comedies have any of the moral significance that Coleridge sees, for example, in Shakespearean comedies— Hazlitt does not mention it. Hazlitt's successors in this tradition follow his form as well as his spirit.

Though Hazlitt's lecture antedates Lamb's criticism of Restoration comedy, Lamb is generally acknowledged as the guiding spirit of the group even by those of his descendants who regard

The *Artificielle* Tradition

him as quaintly simpleminded. While Lamb's style is sometimes as lyrical as his contemporaries' poetry, he sounds almost Johnsonian in his regard for the moral evaluation of literature. "Take one of their characters [from a Restoration comedy], male or female (with few exceptions they are all alike), and place it in a modern play, and my virtuous indignation shall rise against the profligate wretch as warmly as the Catos of the pit could desire; because in a modern play I am to judge of the right and wrong."[2] And Lamb is just as traditional in his attitude toward the morality of the dramatis personae. "Judged morally, every character in these plays—the few exceptions are *mistakes*—is alike essentially vain and worthless" (p. 175). Genial Charles Lamb can enjoy the comedies—and urge contemporary audiences to enjoy them, too—because in no way do they correspond to nineteenth-century London life. No member of the audience or critic "could [ever] connect those sports of a witty fancy in any shape with any result to be drawn from them to imitation of real life. They are a world of themselves almost as much as a fairy land. . . . They have got out of Christendom into the land . . . of cuckoldry—the Utopia of gallantry, where pleasure is duty, and the manners perfect freedom" (pp. 173, 174). Lamb answers Collier's question of "the immorality and profaneness" of Restoration comedy by never really asking it.

By denying any possible connection between Restoration life and his own London life, Lamb can champion "the artificial comedy of the last century," as he calls it. The dissimilarity of the two Londons—Harry Horner's and Abel Magwitch's—ensures the moral safety of the audience. The salutary moral effect results from the fleeting respite from the "real world," the escape which the "artificial" lives of Restoration characters afford the audience. Lamb's essay is an expression of an aesthetics which became increasingly popular in the century, though it is questionable whether Lamb realized the theoretical implications of his essay (certainly his enthusiasm about making moral judgments about modern plays and his reluctance to view Restoration comedy as anything but "artificial" seem contradictory positions). To view the comedies both as anodynes and historically

37

accurate images of their age is a view which Lamb's successor, Leigh Hunt, did not emphasize but which figures prominently in modern criticism, even when modern critics are quick to censure Lamb for his naïve aesthetics.[3]

Leigh Hunt's edition of *The Dramatic Works of Wycherley, Congreve, Vanbrugh, and Farquhar with Biographical and Critical Notices* (1840) is a handsomely printed volume in which the biographical sketches show some evidence of original research, and the critical notices, while brief, are intended to provide "some idea of the moral spirit in which [the plays] deserve to be read."[4] Hunt's notion of the proper "moral spirit" is obviously influenced by Lamb and Hazlitt. Indeed, he reprints *in toto* the essays discussed above at the end of his own critical notice, but he stakes out a position much less extravagant. In the first place, he abjures the self-righteousness of his contemporaries who revile Restoration drama on moral grounds, suggesting that "our ancestors may not have been as bad as we suppose them, even upon our own principles" (p. lxxix).

Hunt is not willing to compromise the contemporary moral code, but he does wish to apply it sympathetically and judiciously. Though he does not mention a Whig interpretation of history, he suspects its existence. By pleading for a "charitable" response to the milieu and characters of the comedies, Hunt declares that the rakes do not always mean what they seem to say. When the readers find a cruel remark, they should realize that the rakes "mean it to the letter as little as anybody"; the proper response is to read the plays "with a grain of allowance,—and a tendency to go away with as much of it for use as is necessary, and the rest for the luxury of laughter, pity, or poetical admiration" (p. lxxix). In short, the reader should approach the plays charitably, seeing them as they are (which Hunt says Lamb failed to do) and "correcting" them as one goes. A reader deficient in such magnanimity, Hunt feels, cannot be "helped" by Restoration comedy. "If you feel neither generous nor blithe in the perusal, neither moved to correct the letter of the worst passages by the spirit of the best, nor to feel that the whole has some healthy end beyond itself, thus mistrusting the final purposes

The *Artificielle* Tradition

and good-nature of Nature herself, as they operate through the medium of a lively art, you may certainly need restraints which these holiday-going dramatists are as certainly not in a condition to supply" (p. lxxxi). His touchstones thus become generosity and blithe spirit, traits as much a property of the plays as they are a desideratum of the ideal reader.

Returning to a defense which Dennis had employed 150 years earlier, Hunt somehow makes the putative moral defects of the plays into symptoms of a poor reader's diseased sensibility. Readers and critics hostile to the comedies "assumed that the writers were so many knaves and fiends, who had positively malignant intentions; and in so doing, [Collier] was not aware that he betrayed a vice in his own spirit, which if they had thought as ill of it as he did of their licence, would have warranted them in denouncing him as the far greater devil of the two. For to believe in such unmitigated wickedness at all, is itself the worst part of the result of vice; namely, a moral melancholy and an attribution to the Creator of having made what he never did" (p. lxxxi). As a cure for moral melancholy, Restoration comedy is a godsend. While Lamb is invigorated by a richly embroidered fantasy world, Hunt's spirits are raised by the buoyant gaiety of the comedies. "If the stage at that time was one half licentious, in the other half it was not only innocent of all evil intention, [it] had a sort of gaiety in the very gaiety of its trust in nature" (p. lxxxii). Whoever finds Restoration comedy patently offensive, says Hunt, has held up a mirror to his own deformity. Charitably approached, the comedies are delightful.

Though aware of the potentially licentious element in the plays, Hunt argues nevertheless that the cumulative effect of the comedies on a healthy sensibility is beneficial. However reluctant he was to recommend the plays for children or as a guide to conduct in his own age (p. lxxx), he is sufficiently confident of their value to his age that he will not brook the "mutilated editions" (i.e., Bowdlerized editions) so popular with his peers.[5] Since he concludes his "critical notice" by reprinting Lamb and Hazlitt's essays and indicates his approval of Hazlitt's, Hunt endorses the "artificial" approach as the "moral spirit" in which the plays

39

should be read. To his disappointment and his publisher's chagrin, his edition of the Restoration comedies became the target of Macaulay's furious denouncement in the *Edinburgh Review* only three months after publication. But the "artificial" approach did not die with Hunt's abortive attempt to modify Victorian taste or with Macaulay's fulmination, for John Palmer revived it in 1913 and made its aesthetic principles fashionable once more.

The title of Palmer's study, *The Comedy of Manners*, implies the author's interest in Restoration "manners." Adding only Etherege to the four playwrights Hunt included in his edition of 1840 (not of 1849 as Palmer frequently states),[6] Palmer strives vigorously to rehabilitate the reputation of and revive interest in the Restoration comic dramatists. But he also offers a more thorough consideration of the relation between drama and morality than is found in the nineteenth-century critics. Despite his denial of the "art for art's sake" dictum, his argument about the morality of these comedies seems as much indebted to the *fin de siècle* aesthetics as to Lamb. Speaking particularly of Etherege at one point, Palmer elevates "sincerity" to a high moral status and evaluates, it seems, the ethical properties of the creative act rather than what is created. Etherege, for example, was

> a man who in temperament and mind accurately reflected this period in his personal character, and received a sincere impulse to reflect it artistically in his comedies. His sincerity as an artist has met the inevitable reward. His plays are morally as well as artistically sound. The result of his honesty and purity of motive as an artist is that, as soon as we enter the imaginative regions of his comedy, we are sensible that the laws are harmonious and just; they will bear inspection. We are sensible of a strange land; but it does not occur to us to question the finality of its laws so long as we remain within its bounds. They are not laws with which we are familiar to-day in the homes of Kensington or Mayfair; but having submitted our imagination to the author in the act of consenting to read his comedy, that suggestion can only intrude when the comedy is put away. Moreover, when the comedy is put away, we are aware that the morality of this strange country, just because Etherege was an artist sincerely endeavouring to see life and express it, has a positive value of its own. (P. 292)

The *Artificielle* Tradition

Palmer's criticism of Etherege brings up three major points. First, Palmer joins Lamb in positing a "strange land" in which ordinary moral judgments are irrelevant, obviated by the very nature of the agreement between author and audience. The fictional world of Restoration comedy has no resemblance to the world Palmer knows—or that Lamb and Hazlitt knew—but the fictional cosmos is internally consistent and therefore admirable. Second, Palmer's critical touchstone is his discovery of the author's sincerity (the word is used three times in the quotation above) or purity of emotion. Palmer does not reveal how to penetrate the artifice of the comedies to discover the author's motives or how to judge a work whose author seems insincere. His thesis is circular: the fictional world is satisfactory to him, so the author must have been sincere; a sincere artist produces only satisfactory fictions. Third, Palmer's final statement suggests that any phase of human experience that is realized imaginatively has a positive value. Regardless of the ethos of the "strange country," any sincere attempt to portray imaginatively this strange world has a positive value. Literature is moral if it is produced by a sincere imagination.

Even when Palmer regards the characters in Congreve's plays as "lecherous young men and incontinent young women" (p. 14), he does not consider them immoral in the usual sense of the word. On the contrary, his central argument is that the immoral characters exist quite properly in their fictional worlds and in no way impinge on or conflict with the moral life of an ordinary reader. "To suggest that Mr. Horner is a wicked man is not to suggest that his conduct might conceivably be improved. The suggestion utterly destroys him. As soon as we attempt to drag him before the expert moral tribunal of Collier and Steele, Mr. Horner turns to simple moonshine. The tribunal is left to pass judgment upon a wraith" (p. 9). For Palmer, as for the aesthetes of the *fin de siècle,* works of art are wholly autonomous. The reader's moral sense is altogether extraneous to the reader's imaginative engagement in a fictional world. In a more complex way the reader restates Lamb's thesis and echoes Wilde's.

Palmer's last chapter most vigorously presents his aesthetic principles, for we learn there that the artist, to use traditional metaphors, is both a mirror and a lamp. On one hand the artist does mirror his age: it is, after all, "an honest reflexion of contemporary manners" (p. 15) that we find in Restoration drama. On the other hand the artist's sincerity enables him to transcend the ephemera of time and circumstance and the parochial morality of a particular society. Attacking Collier's notions of morality as ossified and oppressive, Palmer asserts that

> If by morality is understood the minutiae of the contemporary code, then obviously bad morality may be not only good art but better manners. But there is a higher morality than that of Jeremy Collier—a plane upon which Plato and St. Francis, Confucius and Elijah may meet. . . . A great artist does not consciously intend to be a great prophet. His prophesying comes by the way. His impulse is to create imaginatively in the likeness of things felt and seen; but precisely in proportion to the strength of his artistic impulse he sees clearer and feels deeper into life than common folk. He aims at winning from the chaos of life one more province for the imagination of man; but the province when put upon the map is perceived to be in the loftiest sense a moral as well as an imaginative triumph. (P. 290)

Palmer's ultimate defense of Restoration comedy rests on Neoplatonic and romantic assumptions that the artist has access to a realm of morality in which truth, implicitly defined by Palmer as the reflection of society by a sincere man, is beauty and beauty truth. Insofar as the artist becomes a luminous reflector, his work is moral and the reader may participate pleasurably and safely in his "strange world."

Somewhat less exuberant and more scholarly than Palmer's rehabilitative study are two critical studies published a decade later, Bonamy Dobrée's *Restoration Comedy* (1924) and Kathleen Lynch's *The Social Mode of Restoration Comedy* (1926). Both works deal with the relation of drama and society and trace the development of the comedy of manners, for by this time Palmer's phrase, though it did not originate with him, had been reified into a taxonomic tag. When they discuss the morality of the manners, however, their methods differ. Dobrée is an "appreciative" critic, striving to arouse interest in the comic drama. When

The *Artificielle* Tradition

he touches the moral issue, he treats it as a literary curiosity, an oddity which no longer merits consideration.

> Does not the whole question of impurity, and any attempt to justify it, seem a little absurd? For even if we abhor the idea of sexual looseness in real life, this does not preclude the possibility of turning the common facts of life into art. . . . If we are disgusted at the "impurities" which are the material of much of this comedy, are they handled with sufficient skill to make us indifferent to the subject matter? Or is there, in spite of much that disgusts us, enough beauty and intelligence to overbalance our revulsion in favour of delight? Or can we simply accept the life of the time, and without associating it with ourselves, derive interest and pleasure from the observation and understanding of men whose outlook on life died with their erring bodies some centuries ago?[7]

Dobrée's questions are rhetorical. "Surely," he replies, "this seems the reasonable answer" (p. 26). His list of questions commingles various kinds of arguments, though none unfamiliar to critics in the *artificielle* tradition. First, he regards any concern with "impurity" as juvenile, if not atavistic. More important, he perceives a dichotomy between the content (however base or disgusting) and its expression (which can transform the content into a thing of beauty). Third, Dobrée offers a plea for aesthetic and moral relativism: to enjoy the plays, one must create temporarily a sympathetic outlook on ideas and customs long since discarded even if that "sympathetic outlook" is radically inconsistent with one's sensibility.

But what is this "Restoration outlook" that supposedly expired at the end of the seventeenth century? It is the moral code of the *honnête homme,* a fusion of French libertinism, native English skepticism, Hobbesian materialism, and Machiavellian pragmatism. The Restoration outlook reflects historical conditions in an unflinchingly realistic way: Dobrée spends several pages on historical analogues of comic scenes, hoping to show that the plays faithfully reproduce situations and events of Restoration society. The playwrights' fidelity to real life enables the modern reader to glimpse the distinctive morality of these plays.

CRITICS, VALUES, AND RESTORATION COMEDY

> If we were to try to sum up what the comedy . . . achieved, it would be to say that it gave a brilliant picture of its time rather than a new insight into man. . . . Their time forced them to be too critical, though it is hardly fair to blame a time for the very peculiarities that gave them their best material. But they were forced to be too moral, that is, too engaged with the immediate application of their ideas. It is in this sense that the word moral has been used throughout: nothing so foolish is suggested as that art and morality are incompatible, any more than that they are necessary to one another. . . . But the morality of the Restoration dramatists was not a universal vision; it could not be. For the medieval view was dead, had died in the iron verse of Milton; eighteenth-century scepticism was being born, had made its appearance in the shattering syllogisms of Hobbes and the trenchant strokes of Shaftesbury. Modern curiosity was awakening, and the old moral order lay in ruins about the scaffold of a king. The dramatists of that day were almost necessarily forced to be content with morality as conceived by the *honnête homme*. (pp. 171, 172)

Dobrée's notions about literary history are perfectly intelligible within the *moralisé* tradition, though one could challenge the historical accuracy of the scenario on which it is partially based. His constellation of arguments covers familiar ground: Restoration comedy faithfully reflects the *Zeitgeist* of contemporary society, one which has disappeared but has left us a legacy of empiricism ("modern curiosity was awakening") and secular humanism ("the old moral order lay in ruins"). Milton's brand of Christianity was bound and gagged by his iron verse whereas Hobbes and Shaftesbury emancipated England from an outmoded ethics and epistemology. Since modern curiosity was nascent and since one of the areas about which man was most curious was sex, Restoration comedy expresses "not licentiousness, but a deep curiosity, and a desire to try new ways of living" (p. 22). Though he seems headed toward a position inimical to Palmer's or Lamb's—he seems to laud the moral content of Restoration comedy—Dobrée reverses himself in summarizing the proper way to regard the plays.

Despite his endorsement of the classic *artificielle* position that Restoration morality need not impede our enjoyment of Resto-

The *Artificielle* Tradition

ration art (the reasonable attitude, after all, is "to accept the life of the times, and without associating it with ourselves, derive interest and pleasure from the observation of men whose outlook on life died"), Dobrée concludes by praising the ethos of these comedies. Earlier in the study, however, he had written of "free comedy" (i.e., Restoration comedy) in the same airy language which Lamb, Hazlitt, or Palmer might have used.

> Here we feel that no values count, that there are no rules of conduct, hardly laws of nature. Certainly no appeal, however indirect, is made to our critical or moral faculties. We can disport ourselves freely in a realm where nothing is accountable; all we need to exact is that the touch shall be light enough. . . . Judgement, except the aesthetic, is out of place here. We are permitted to play with life, which becomes a charming harlequinade without being farce. It is all spontaneous and free, rapid and exhilirating; the least emotion, an appeal to common sense, and the joyous illusion is gone. (P. 14)

Clearly, this passage excludes the moral sense from the aesthetic judgment even though Dobrée later insists that the moral sense should be satisfied by the content of the plays. In essence, Dobrée fuses two contradictory critical positions. Like Lamb, he postulates the existence of a morally neutral aesthetic experience, an imaginative perception of a comic world in which moral values neither affect nor matter to the audience after the comedy concludes. But he also insists that the comedies "mean" something significant outside the theatre; their ideas and their moral vision signify the modern world view at its creation. If nothing else, Dobrée has successfully eluded that hobgoblin of little minds on the important issue of how the plays affect the audience.

Lynch's criticism begins with warm praise for Palmer's work, for she considers his study of "manners" a wholly satisfactory working definition of Restoration comedy.[8] She then charts the emergence of the comedy of manners from Elizabethan comedy, Caroline court comedy, and the comic drama of the Commonwealth. Her conclusions about the comedy of manners are not surprising, given her initial assumptions: but what Palmer and

Lamb had praised—the "artificial" aesthetic experience—Lynch sees as a limitation.

> Beyond the art of Congreve, Restoration comedy of manners could not advance. Its essential excellences and its essential limitations were completely realized in his work. In brilliant dialogue, in vivid contrasts of social types, in the expression of that eager, yet formal urbanity of temper which characterized Restoration society at its best, Congreve triumphed over all other comic dramatists of his age. It was his further distinction to reveal clearly how inexpressive such comedy must be of the realities of character, how profound must be its silences concerning human passions, how restrained and stereotyped must remain its rule of life.... [The comedy has appeal] not only as a picturesque literary phenomenon of a special era, but also as an interpretation of a type of comic predicament perpetually recurring in civilized society, whenever the lives of men and women become dominated by artificial standards of social discipline. (P. 217)

The achievement of Restoration comedy is its verbal texture, which limns clearly the artificial social comedy of Restoration life; its chief limitation is the superficiality of the characters, which, paradoxically, is another way of explaining their appeal to the *artificielle* critics. The plays are literary antiques, valuable for the passionless experience that results from studying them. Whether the plays contain themes or ideas that engage the reader's passions or celebrate some values and censure others, Lynch does not say. Her emphasis in such an "influence" study might preclude discussion of such matters, but her admiration of Palmer's analysis is a more likely explanation for this curious lacuna. She concludes about Congreve, for example, that his plays present "a brief, authentic record of the *précieuse* movement in comedy" (p. 212); about Etherege, the only other dramatist discussed in detail, she asserts that "every fresh reading of *The Man of Mode* leaves with us a renewed sense of the *précieuse* influence in Etherege's comedy" (p. 181). One would gather that the plays are of no more intellectual or moral significance, say, than a scented periwig. While her contemporary, Mr. Dobrée, had waf-

The *Artificielle* Tradition

fled on the issue, Lynch is as silent as Lamb or Hazlitt on this matter.

In another historical study written nearly forty years after Lynch's book, Sarup Singh considers the theory of drama in the Restoration. After surveying seventeenth-century theories of heroic drama, poetic justice, opera, tragicomedy, and the unities, he turns to the comedy of manners and distinguishes sharply between "humours comedy," which has a traditional moral purpose, and the comedy of manners, which strives only to be entertaining. Dryden's Preface to *An Evening's Love* seems to make this distinction and insists as well that the demands for poetic justice need not be observed as strictly in comedy as in tragedy: "the chief end of [comedy] is divertisement and delight: and that so much, that it is disputed, I think, by Heinsius, before Horace his *Art of Poetry*, whether instruction be any part of its employment. At least I am sure it can be but its secondary end: for the business of the poet is to make you laugh: when he writes humour, he makes folly ridiculous; when wit, he moves you, if not always to laughter, yet to a pleasure that is more noble."[9]

Dryden's remark is only one of numerous opinions about the aesthetics of the comedy of manners,[10] but Singh states that it was "more or less acceptable to the whole age" (p. 214). But after devoting fifty pages to a discussion of the interplay of wit, humour, and realism in the comedy of manners, Singh pauses momentarily to describe more fully what he imagines was a contemporary understanding of the "manners" genre and thus what historical critics should strive to re-create through their criticism.

> This comedy postulated "an ideal life of wit, gallantry, and pleasure." As far as possible it allowed nothing to intrude into this "ideal" world, nothing crudely realistic, moral or sentimental, nothing, in fact, which might cast a doubt over its artificiality. Here "reality" was almost "anesthetised". The action often seemed to have no time or place and the characters and their acts no subsequent or consequent life or value. Here indeed was a complete holiday from life and all that it stands for: no passion ("Passion" being "the most unbecoming thing in the world", as Lord Foppington declared), no feeling or sentiment,

"altogether a speculative scene of things" (in Charles Lamb's words), "which has no reference whatever to the world that is"). (P. 257)

Singh's position is squarely situated in the *artificielle* camp as he quotes and echoes much of the criticism I have examined in this chapter. His conclusions about the genre attempt to justify on historical grounds the aesthetic experience which Palmer and Lamb had characterized as the proper response to the comedy of manners.

While Lynch had studied seventeenth-century dramaturgy and social traditions to account for the form of the plays, Singh extrapolates from miscellaneous remarks by seventeenth-century dramatists a theory of the comedy of manners that embodies *his* conception of dramatic theory, not necessarily theirs. His assumptions about dramatic theory are supported by short quotations amassed from brief remarks by numerous writers: it is more likely that his conclusions would corroborate Palmer's assumptions than that they would illuminate Restoration comedy. Since it was difficult for a comedy to keep its "purity" unsullied by realism, Singh finds only a few scenes in which "this comedy achieves its highest perfection and seems temporarily to shut out reality," for life, "often unrecognized perhaps, seems to be knocking at the door" (p. 258). His argument and figurative language derive, of course, from the particular branch of the *moralisé* tradition to which he belongs. At least in this chapter on the comedy of manners, Singh's historical criticism becomes an extension of Palmer's "appreciative" criticism.

Like their *réaliste* colleagues, the *artificielle* critics find that Restoration comedy is moral, but their supporting arguments are substantially different. They do not attempt to show that Restoration comedy embodies a traditional world view or that poetic justice is strictly observed; they do not make a broad plea for ethical relativism; they do not argue that the plays deal with the plight of the sensitive self in a rigid and brutal society. They emphasize the remoteness of the plays from the critics' lives, the effervescent splendor of an ancient social code, the vivacity of the characters and their witty dialogue, all of which combine to

The *Artificielle* Tradition

suspend the critics' usual moral judgments and to plunge them into a world where actions have no pertinent causes or significant consequences. Restoration comedy is a two-hour holiday for the spirit, a brief escape from the routine and the dull. That the plays offer the spectator nothing but respite is not only a boon but an indication that the *artificielle* approach most adequately accounts for their response to the plays. The respite is salutary and therefore moral. Opponents of these plays or this approach to them, these critics might say, suffer from what Hunt termed "moral melancholy," a condition whose victims attack Restoration comedies either with the charge of "immorality and profaneness" or with the demand that the plays reflect an Arnoldian moral seriousness. Either approach shreds the gossamer of illusion—the sine qua non of this approach—and destroys the comedies. The *artificielle* critics from Hazlitt to Singh would restore a correct understanding of these comedies by regarding them as Baroque antiques—ornamental, nonutilitarian, fragile, and beautiful when preserved in the pure amber of dramatic illusion.

4

Literature and Moral Persuasion: The Critics' Dilemma

> While modern apologists for humane studies proclaim the benefits derived from literary consumption, Platonic objectors survive; and in truth the effects of literature on the individual and on the collectivity are not well understood even after two and a half millenia of claims and counterclaims.[1]

The analysis of the *moralisé* tradition discloses the variety of critical assumptions and approaches that define the criticism of Restoration comedy. The substantial differences among critics who agree that Restoration comedy is moral reflect quite different ideas on two major questions: in what way or ways can literature be considered moral, and how does literature achieve its moral effects? By examining closely these two contestable concepts, I refine our understanding of the checkered criticism of Restoration comedy and establish the major premises for my criticism of four "problem" comedies in the final two chapters.

Despite their other differences, the critics in the *moralisé* tradition concur that Restoration comedy is moral. But how is it moral, or, more broadly, what does moral mean when it describes a work of literature? Sidney Zink, a philosopher, analyzes the critics' silence on these questions in a way that suggests the need for workable definitions of key terms prior to other aesthetic considerations. "Most critics seem agreed not to ask what the good is. This suggests that, whatever the good may be, the critics will not disagree about it. And that may be because the nature of this thing is either unquestionably clear or impossibly vague. It cannot be that critics are lazy, or feel a philosophical incompetence. And if the nature of the good were impossibly vague, one could not profitably inquire into the efficacy of literature in promoting it. So the subject must be very clear."[2]

The tacit agreement not to discuss "the good" consequently muddles discussion of the relation between Restoration comedy and "the good" it is thought to promote. Furthermore, the referent of "moral"—the acts or attitudes it designates—has become increasingly vague in modern society, perhaps because of what Daniel Bell calls verbal "entropy," a semantic condition in which abstract words that have been overused "mean" nothing unless the user specifies a particular meaning.[3] One recalls Alice's chagrin and confusion upon discovering that in Wonderland words mean anything the speaker desires. Again Zink provides a helpful discrimination. "An initial distinction ought to be made between the questions of art and the good, and of art and the moral. The problems of what is "good" and what is "moral" are distinct: the first consists in the description, definition, and gradation of all significant values; the second in the description of the attitude of the human valuer toward values. . . . The moral attitude is that of conscientious pursuit of the right solution to a moral conflict" (pp. 545–46). This definition of the "good" affirms that for "moral" to be meaningful, it must refer to a coherent ethical system, a comprehensive taxonomy of significant values.

But what if there are competing systems of morality, as there necessarily will be in a pluralistic society? If the description, definition, and gradation of values are fully articulated or if the critic refers to such an articulated system, there should be no confusion about "moral": it refers to an external and coherent scheme of values. It is quite possible to understand an orthodox Christian's or Marxist's use of the word, even if one questions the appropriateness of its application in a particular case. But when Critic A describes *The Country Wife* or *Ulysses* or *Deep Throat* as "moral" or "immoral," he is intelligible only to the extent that he clearly refers to an explicit scheme of values. Without such reference, "moral" signifies nothing except that in some way or for some reason or by some criteria, the critic admires a sentiment, a character, or a theme in a work.

In other words, one way to conclude that a work of art is moral is to weigh the congruence of its moral vision with the values held by the critic. E. M. W. Tillyard postulates that one element of the epic, perhaps almost a choric element, is the capacity of the epic to embody "an accepted unconscious metaphysic of the time."[4] Tillyard's point is more widely applicable than he claims. Since every work of art must reflect a system of values and a way of understanding the forces that affect human events, every critic must inevitably respond to the metaphysic enacted in the work. When the critic concludes that the work is moral, he is signaling approval of what is seen as the moral vision, say, of a Restoration comedy.

But there are other ways for literature to be "moral" besides having a vision that is harmonious with the critic's. Some critics argue that a work is moral not because of its content—whatever that is perceived to be—but because of its effects on the audience. The *artificielle* critics, for example, hold that literature is an anodyne whose moral effect is to distract the audience from its mundane concerns by immersion in a fictive world. While reality is suspended, the spirit rests and is renewed by its respite from the workaday world. Other critics argue that literature, particularly drama, achieves its moral effects through some sort of purgative experience: the classic exposition of tragic theory can be found in Aristotle's *Poetics*, but the definitive statement on comedy is less easily located. The effects of satiric comedy are thought to be moral edification: the audience ridicules the vices and follies of foolish characters or is persuaded to admire and emulate the virtues of wise characters. To ensure that their moral perspective is perceived, some dramatists (Ben Jonson, for example) include choric characters, prologues, and epilogues that underscore either the moral "content" or the effects to be achieved.

If critics of Restoration comedy are vague about acknowledging the ethical values that shape their responses, they are nev-

The Critics' Dilemma

ertheless confident that the experience of reading (or viewing) Restoration comedies has a predictable effect on the reader (or viewer), probably the same effect that the comedies have on the critic. Such critics as Collier, Taine, and Beljame were convinced that Restoration comedies significantly and adversely affected the behavior of their contemporary audience and thus of society. It is not important here to show that their conception of the audience was wrong—Avery, Love, Scouten, Hume, and others have already demonstrated that convincingly[5]—but it is worthwhile to consider their assumption that comedy *can* affect the moral code and behavior of its audience beneficially or perniciously. Although Samuel Johnson, Taine, Beljame, and Macaulay all agree that the comic fare was morally detrimental to English society, the apologists for Restoration comedy should ask whether comedy has such power and can, in fact, demonstrably alter human values or behavior. I have found none, however, who considers the matter in more than a perfunctory manner.

In its broadest form, the argument that literature has an instrumental moral value reflects one of two assumptions. Art can be "considered a means to either private or public improvement, or both, in the sphere of religion, politics, morality, or truth"; or art can be seen as a "unique means to a private or public improvement only if it is first conceived as an end in itself."[6] The debate about the effects of imaginative literature is an ancient one, for Plato disvalued art for the same reason Aristotle valued it: its putative effects on the audience. But this question about the moral effects of art is raised most frequently today in debates not among literary critics but among social scientists and shapers of public policy.

It would be futile to argue that a Restoration comedy was moral or immoral on the basis of its alleged effects on its audience. First of all, the relation of literature to society has not been clearly established. Moreover, the effects of particular works on individual readers are difficult to measure. Even with the research techniques and statistical ingenuity of modern psychology, psychometry, and sociology, the Commission on Obscenity and Pornography found no causal relation between exposure to erotica and changes in the values, attitudes, and behavior of adults.[7] That erotica or classic works of literature seem to evoke powerful changes or create substantial effects in their audience can be glimpsed in the testimony of criminals, saints, and sensitive readers in many ages. But whether literature actually achieves such effects has not been established despite the assiduity of numerous researchers.

Similarly, the research on the effects of television violence on human behavior is not conclusive. In two studies Seymour Feshbach considered the stimulating versus cathartic effect of cinematic violence. In the first study he concluded that "participation in a vicarious aggressive act results in a reduction in subsequent aggressive behavior if aggressive drive has been aroused at the time of such participation; if aggressive drive has not been aroused at the time of participation in a vicarious aggressive act, such participation results in an increase in subsequent aggressive behavior."[8] In other words, under some conditions seeing an aggressive activity (for example, Hamlet's summary execution of Polonius) stimulates some people to behave aggressively; under other conditions, the same people are not stimulated. Ten years later Feshbach and Roger Singer reported that

> exposure to aggressive content in television over a six-week period does not produce an increment in aggressive behavior. . . . The results, in fact, indicate that witnessing aggressive TV programs reduces rather than stimulates the acting out of aggressive tendencies in certain types of boys. . . . What is most compelling about the data is the regularity with which the obtained differences in aggressive behaviors and changes in aggressive attitudes and values point to a reducing or controlling rather than to a stimulating or disinhibiting effect of exposure to aggressive interaction in television programs.[9]

What seems clear from the studies of aggression is that different people respond to stimuli in different ways at different times. While some generalizations apply to most people much of the time, human difference will not support absolute statements

The Critics' Dilemma

that claim to predict human response to art, whether erotica or televised violence or the bedroom banter of *The London Cuckolds*. Even with the depth of social concern about such problems as the moral effects of pornography and violence, no unequivocal guides can be found among the social scientists of our age. The problem for the apologist who wishes to defend Restoration comedies because of their moral effects is to demonstrate that the comedies create certain desirable effects or arouse certain desirable responses.

The treatment of this ancient problem in literary criticism, while not specifically directed toward Restoration comedy, may reveal the intellectual boundaries of rival theories in two important ways: the competing theories of how literature "works" heavily influence the approaches taken by the *moralisé* critics; and a proper understanding of the aspects of this problem may illuminate the difficulties inherent in an ethical response to literature. By looking closely at critics in what I term "the great tradition" and their modern successors, I identify and clarify the intellectual underpinnings of the *moralisé* critics.

There are at least two strategies by which critics attempt to persuade their readers that experiencing a literary work is beneficial to the individual and thus to society. The first way is for the critic to align himself with and appeal to the authority of the great tradition, critics ancient and modern, who proclaimed the salutary power of art. The second way is to attempt to "prove" that the work produces these desirable effects. The first approach is venerable, and reference to the great tradition summons the collective wisdom of the most distinguished ancients (Aristotle, Horace, Cicero, and Longinus) and many of the moderns (Sidney, Dryden, Johnson, and Arnold). The particular contribution of each critic is not important here; it is sufficient to observe the existence of this tradition and consider its pervasive influence and authority as one reads, for example, Northrop Frye's pronouncement on the power of literature near the end of his *Anatomy of Criticism*. "There is no reason why a great poet should be a wise and good man, or even a tolerable human being, but there is every reason why *his reader should be improved in his humanity* [emphasis is mine] as a result of reading him. Hence while the production of culture may be, like ritual, a half-involuntary imitation of organic rhythms or processes, the response to culture is, like myth, a revolutionary act of consciousness."[10] What exactly does Frye mean by "improved in his humanity"? His language confers the highest praise on literature but is neither clarified nor supported by any hint of how such a claim might be substantiated.

In a similar vein, T. S. Eliot characterizes his assumptions about the power of literature to alter attitudes and behavior. "Our religion imposes our ethics, our judgment and criticism of ourselves, and our behavior toward our fellow men. The fiction that we read affects our behavior towards our fellow men, affects our patterns of ourselves. When we read of human beings behaving in certain ways, with the approval of the author, who gives his benediction to this behavior by his attitude toward the result of the behavior arranged by himself, we can be influenced towards behaving in the same way."[11]

While neither Frye nor Eliot suggests evidence to support his claims, this should be no surprise to readers familiar with the lineaments of the great tradition, which has for two millenia proclaimed the power of literature to engineer, in Frye's words, "a revolutionary act of consciousness." This power is the seductive power of poetry that Stephen Gosson so feared that he could characterize it only by *anadiplosis*: from poetry, readers are led to piping, "from pyping to playing, from play to pleasure, from pleasure to slouth, from slouth to sleepe, from sleepe to sinne, from sinne to death, from death to the Divel."[12] These linguistic dominoes disregarded, the position is analogous to the positions of Frye and Eliot. Whatever their disagreements on other aesthetic, political, and moral matters, the critics in the great tradition uniformly affirm the potency of literature to alter what people believe and how they act. After looking briefly at five major representatives of the great tradition, I will then consider an alternative strategy proposed by modern theorists, whose argument that literature inculcates moral values either is based on a psychological model of aesthetic experience and psychological

The Critics' Dilemma

change or involves clinical and thus "scientific" self-scrutiny of their own experience of literature. If it seems that Restoration comedy and its critics have been forgotten amid the historical background, it must be remembered that the critics' responses to the comedies presuppose particular ways of valuing literature, of seeing it as moral, and of making critical judgments based upon their responses.

Aristotle's synoptic interest in the passions, rhetoric, and ethics almost makes the subjects inseparable. One could make a good case for reading the *Rhetoric* and the *Poetics* as separate chapters of the same work. After analyzing the passions and their vulnerability to the skillful orator in the *Rhetoric*,[13] Aristotle discusses them again in the *Poetics*, this time presenting a psychological theory of fear and pity as components of the aesthetic experience. Two matters are especially pertinent: first, he presents an implicit apology for poetry by discussing its instrumental value to society (poetry siphons off emotional excesses, as Dennis was to argue two millennia later and as Feshbach partially documented three centuries after that),[14] and he bases his aesthetic dicta about tragedy on the assumption that art affects the audience in a uniform and predictable manner. He takes for granted that tragedies elicit a uniform response from the audience and in no way attempts to prove logically or test analytically this assumption despite his interest in logical and scientific inquiry.

In the form we have it, the *Poetics* is not just a miscellany of prescriptive notions about epic and tragedy. It is also a shrewd analysis of why works succeed or fail. I cite this mixture of psychological speculation and keen literary insight because it sets an important precedent: from Aristotle to the modern critics, one finds a priori assumptions about the effects of art central to defenses of particular works (e.g., *The Country Wife*) or of art in general. Even a cursory glance at Sidney, Dryden, Johnson, and Arnold should sufficiently illustrate this point and illuminate this aspect of the *moralisé* tradition. For all of these critics, literature pleases the spectators and holds their attention by the vividness or forcefulness of the imitation, and it instructs because it is an exemplary illustration of the consequences of moral values and acts. Few critics before the twentieth century seriously challenge the assumption that literature should or can "instruct" in this way.

For Sidney, poetry is "that fayning notable images of vertues, vices, or what els, with that delightfull teaching, which must be the right describing note to know a Poet by."[15] The poet's representation of the virtues and the vices is more efficacious than the philosopher's because it "yeeldeth to the powers of the minde an image of that whereof the Philosophere bestoweth but a woordish description: which dooth neyther strike, pierce, nor possesse the sight of the soule so much as that other dooth" (p. 164). Philosophical truths "lye dark before the imaginatiue and iudging powre, if they bee not illuminated or figured forth by the speaking picture of Poesie" (p. 165). Just how the speaking picture "strikes," "pierces," and "possesses" the sight of the soul is a matter of as much interest to students of Renaissance psychology, philosophy, and aesthetics as to modern aestheticians who make similar claims in somewhat different language. Like Aristotle, Sidney predicates his argument on an assumption about the uniformity of human sensibility, a sensibility that can unerringly detect both the virtuous and the vicious in art and in life. Sidney carries on the great tradition by restating and extending the Aristotelian-Platonic synthesis of aesthetic and ethical concerns, assuming a concordance "of quite different kinds of excellence: the excellence of [literature] as [literature] and the excellence of [literature] as therapy."[16]

As a working dramatist and critic, Dryden endorses orthodox claims about the moral effects of literature. But in the Preface to *An Evening's Love* he argues that the chief end of comedy is "divirtisement and delight" and that instruction is but a secondary aim. If comic drama reforms its audience, it does so not by attacking Vice but by chastising follies,

> for the business of the poet is to make you laugh: when he writes humour, he makes folly ridiculous; when wit, he moves you, if not always to laughter, yet to a pleasure that is more noble. And if he

The Critics' Dilemma

works a cure on folly, and the small imperfections in mankind, by exposing them to public view, that cure is not performed by an immediate operation. For it works first on the ill nature of the audience; they are moved to laugh by the representation of deformity; and the shame of that laughter teaches us to amend what is ridiculous in our manners.[17]

Dryden argues that comedy achieves its didactic aim by providing negative *exempla*, and to underscore his point he uses the language of medicine ("cure," "operation," "deformity"). Just as tragedy achieved its reform through catharsis, comedy flushes out the foolish inclinations of the audience. Like his predecessors in this tradition, Dryden offers the principle of moral instruction as an ipse dixit. Whether drama actually achieves this end or could achieve this end seems not to concern that side of Dryden moderately interested in the empirical investigations of the Royal Society. Thus his critical theory and procedure on this matter differ little from the earlier models.

Samuel Johnson, the greatest of the eighteenth-century critics, articulates for his century the key elements of the *moralisé* tradition. Following the earlier critics, he insists in his *Preface to Shakespeare* that literature can shape our behavior by its forceful representation of general nature. Shakespeare's moral effects result not from the beauty and aptness of his *sententiae* but from "the progress of his fable, and the tenour of his dialogue."[18] Indeed, from Shakespeare's works "may be collected a system of civil and oeconomical prudence" (p. 62). His fidelity to general nature allows him to embody moral and psychological truths that are at once "general, rational, and normative."[19] Like Aristotle, Sidney, and Dryden, Johnson does not consider that a piece of literature may be perceived in radically different ways by different spectators (Johnson's profoundly emotional response to the death of Cordelia is more extreme than most readers') and thus may affect spectators in quite different ways. Johnson's use of general nature makes explicit what was implicit in but not articulated by earlier critics, all of whom combine what M. H. Abrams calls the "mimetic" and "pragmatic" theories of art.[20] What Johnson says of Shakespeare might serve as a touchstone for this approach. "This therefore is the praise of Shakespeare, that his drama is the mirrour of life; that he who has mazed his imagination, in following the phantoms which other writers raise up before him, may here be cured of his delirious extasies, by reading human sentiments in human language; by scenes from which a hermit may estimate the transactions of the world, and a confessor predict the progress of the passions" (p. 65). Shakespeare's excellence in this area is not only his greatest source of moral value but, paradoxically, the occasion for his most grievous flaw. His genius enables him to touch our hearts; his judgment does not always allow him to move them properly.

This is not as paradoxical as it might initially appear. Johnson's repeated insistence that the "greatest graces of a play are to copy nature and instruct life" allows him to praise or censure Shakespeare by referring to the lineaments of general nature. It should not be surprising to notice which is the first of Shakespeare's defects cited in the Preface.

> His first defect is that to which may be imputed most of the evil in books or in men. He sacrifices virtue to convenience, and is so much more careful to please than to instruct, that he seems to write without any moral purpose. From his writings indeed a system of social duty may be selected, for he who thinks reasonably must think morally; but his precepts and axioms drop casually from him; he makes no just distribution of good and evil, nor is always careful to shew in the virtuous a disapprobation of the wicked; he carries his persons indifferently through right and wrong, and at the close dismisses them without further care, and leaves their examples to operate by chance. This fault the barbarity of his age cannot extenuate; for it is always a writer's duty to make the world better, and justice is a virtue independent of time and place. (P. 71)

Johnson finds the deaths of Cordelia and Ophelia unnecessary aesthetically and therefore unsound morally, and he regrets that many passages are vitiated by gratuitous cruelty or sensationalism. Though sensitive to the formal criteria regularly employed in neoclassic dramatic criticism, Johnson gives preeminence to the moral issues.

The Critics' Dilemma

One could speculate, as Hagstrum and others have done, on which elements in Johnson's disposition led to such emphasis on the moral obligations of the playwright, but it is sufficient to state that Johnson, like most critics of his age, was an absolutist and so his literary judgments are ultimately grounded in his metaphysics.[21] In *The Life of Milton* he remarked that "some truths are too important to be new"; these truths are ones which the dramatist cannot ignore or forsake if he wishes "to please many or please long."

Despite his lack of sympathy for neoclassicism in general and Johnson in particular, René Wellek accurately describes Johnson's a priori critical standards as he outlines the general assumptions of English neoclassicism, which recognized "a stable psychology of human nature, a fundamental set of norms in the works themselves, a uniform working of human sensibility and intelligence allowing us to reach conclusions which would be valid for all art and all literature."[22] At no time was Johnson interested in testing empirically the validity of his assumptions despite his capacity for reflective self-examination and probing introspection in other parts of his criticism. His impatience with epistemological innovators like Bishop Berkeley is recorded by Boswell in the famous stone-kicking refutation. For Johnson it would have been vain and trifling to test what all men know to be true of themselves and of all mankind.

Even as Johnson was arguing for the tenets of English neoclassicism, some of his contemporaries were becoming increasingly interested in systematic investigations of aesthetic issues and their concomitant psychological and philosophical implications. The work of such critics as Edmund Burke and the Wartons led, in Lovejoy's phrase, to the "substitution of . . . diversitarianism for uniformitarianism as the ruling preconception in most of the normative provinces of thought."[23] Rather than subscribing to Imlac's dictum that the duty of the poet was not to number the streaks of the tulip, followers of the ascendant aesthetics gloried in the uniqueness of every flower, both weed and rose, in the garden. Lovejoy's description of the new sensibility is pertinent not only as a guide to the assumptions of romantic criticism and thus as a sharp contrast to Johnson's values; it also describes the kind of romantic sensibility that Arnold sought to correct through literature near the end of the century. Lovejoy observes that

> there have, in the entire history of thought, been few changes in standards of value more profound and more momentous than that which took place . . . when it came to be believed not only that in many, or in all phases of human life there are diverse excellences, but that diversity itself is of the essence of excellence; and that of art, in particular, the objective is neither the attainment of some single ideal perfection of form in a small number of fixed *genres* nor the gratification of that least common denominator of aesthetic susceptibility which is shared by all mankind in all ages, but rather the fullest possible expression of the abundance of differentness that there is, actually or potentially, in nature and human nature, and—for the function of the artist in relation to his public—the evocation of capacities for understanding, sympathy, enjoyment, which are as yet latent in most men, and perhaps never capable of universalization. (P. 293)

Despite the abandonment of general nature as a moral and aesthetic norm, romantic critics and poets, in Shelley's famous phrase, continued to see poets as the unacknowledged legislators of mankind. It was Arnold, born in the year Shelley died, who saw most clearly the implications of this new aesthetics when it was fused with the old belief in the sacerdotal power of poetry to transform human lives.

Arnold's *Culture and Anarchy* (1869) is the clearest and most famous of his political essays. Identifying the preservation of culture with the preeminence of "right reason" and wisdom, Arnold views anarchy, like Pope's Dulness, as the antithesis of culture. The spirit of anarchy is sustained less by a philosophical system inimical to British democracy than by a sensibility of, in Arnold's phrase, "doing as one likes." Arnold defines culture and the internecine struggle to preserve it in these terms: "Now, if culture, which simply means trying to perfect oneself, and one's mind as part of oneself, brings us light, and if light shows us that there is nothing so very blessed in merely doing as one likes, that the worship of the mere freedom to do as one likes is worship of machinery, that the really blessed thing is to like what right reason ordains and to follow her authority, then we have got a practical benefit out of culture. We have got a much wanted principle, a principle of authority, to counteract the tendency to anarchy which seems to be threatening us."[24] Elsewhere Arnold had argued that an academy might provide an authoritative judge of excellence in what was thought and said,[25] but since the creation of an academy was unlikely, where was authority to be found? Arnold placed his trust in literature.

"The Study of Poetry" is as interesting as a personal credo as a work of criticism. Arnold's indictment of eighteenth-century poetry reflects Victorian biases, and his praise of the Greek and Roman classics and Shakespeare is equally predictable. What makes great poetry important, however, and "explains" not only the greatness of Homer and Shakespeare but the impotence of Dryden, Pope, and Gray is its truth and seriousness, moral properties that make possible a criticism of life. In a paragraph that T. S. Eliot was to censure harshly, Arnold argues that poetry will take over the responsibilities traditionally held by religion.

> The future of poetry is immense, because in poetry, where it is worthy of its high destinies, our race, as time goes on, will find an even surer and surer stay. There is not a creed which is not shaken, not an accredited dogma which is not shown to be questionable, not a received tradition which does not threaten to dissolve. Our religion has materialised itself in the fact, in the supposed fact; it has attached its emotion to the fact, and now the fact is failing it. But for poetry the idea is everything; the rest is a world of illusion, of divine illusion. Poetry attaches its emotion to the idea; the idea *is* the fact. The strongest part of our religion to-day is its unconscious poetry.[26]

Arnold contended in his later writing that the truth of Scripture was in its poetry, notably in his *Literature and Dogma* (1873) and its defense, *God and the Bible* (1875). Arnold's essay on the moral value of poetry anticipates his later religious views, influenced substantially by liberal German theology and the Higher Criticism, as he places poetry at the heart of religion—the rest of religion is illusion, even if "divine" illusion.

For Arnold poetry is the medium by which religious truths and classical wisdom are preserved and transmitted. Classical literature will be gleaned for its high moral seriousness just as Scripture has been read. Arnold does not mention how one settles disagreements on ethical questions among the great heroes of the Judeo-Christian literary past, but surely it is important whether one drags an enemy by the heels behind a chariot or forgives him. Arnold's faith in a syncretistic and redemptive wisdom—in a literature that *instructs*—is so profound that he does not question the premises of his faith, namely, the power of literature to shape human conduct. While he accords to literature powers and duties that earlier critics in the great tradition would not have granted, his assumptions about the power and the glory of literature are familiar.

In short, one can say that a critical tradition from Aristotle to Arnold, including some of the most important critical voices of our literary heritage, stipulates that literature can and should shape human conduct. The collective weight and insight of these critics notwithstanding, it is clear that one of the key elements in their claims about literature was never subjected to serious question, much less to actual testing. The hypothesis about the power of literature to alter human conduct is reflected as clearly in those who proclaim the power of literature to "improve our humanity" as in those who decry the danger in some kinds of writing. But even in our century there has been no conclusive examination of whether and how literature affects the moral beliefs and behavior of its audience.[27]

Some modern critics who make moral judgments about Restoration comedy inherit the critical language and a priori principles of the great tradition. When John Palmer rejects the "mirror" model for a different kind of psychological model (Restoration comedy is moral because it "releases" the mind from its fretful preoccupation with the world), he has in mind a definite conception of how comedy affects the audience, and yet he retains the central assumption of the great tradition: literature does achieve a salutary and moral effect. While it might be tempting to exaggerate the differences, say, between Palmer and Arnold, it would be equally easy to overlook how much they have in common. Thus, I contend not only that much modern criticism of Restoration comedy reflects the unexamined assumptions about literature of earlier critics but also that some critics, influenced by the "scientific" bias of such critics as I. A. Richards, have abandoned the rhetorical stance of critics who confidently proclaimed their critical truths to be self-evident.

> It is in the world, however, that art must find its level. It must vindicate its function in the human commonwealth. What direct acceptable contribution does it make to the highest good? (Santayana, *Reason in Art*)

Santayana's question succinctly frames the problem that modern critics have been reluctant to consider. As stated, the question seems answerable on empirical grounds. The discovery of the distinctive value of literature in modern society, whether couched in terms of moral instruction or in such language as "enlargement of sympathy," should not elude those critics who hope to offer a convincing apology. But little work has been done in this area. Sidney Zink focuses on the moral effect of art as the locus of its primary contribution to what Santayana terms "the highest good."

> Is it in the nature of art to cause either the moral or its opposite, and, if it can achieve such precepts and habits as the above, is this result an essentially moral one? . . . [There] are records of both criminal and humanitarian actions which have—according to the "appreciators'" confessions—resulted from the appreciation of a work of art. This puts the matter on the basis of fact; and if it were to be settled in this way, we should need a corps of sociologists to conduct a survey and determine whether the vicious or the virtuous results predominate. The philosopher, however, can reject this method on the grounds that the statistician cannot determine whether the contact with art (which is followed by virtue or vice) is an aesthetic contact.[28]

For Zink, art is moral not because it provides "moral answers" but because it forces the audience to grapple with difficult questions of ethics and moral values. Consequently, he defines the aesthetic experience as "a conscientiousness of mind and will in the scrutiny and actualization of values" (p. 556). Despite his contempt for the methods of sociologists—Zink would consign them to the island of Laputa—his own approach is hardly more workable. In fact, he reverts to the methodology of the great tradition, stipulating that a particular mental condition is aroused by specific works of art (in his case, tragedy) and that this condition is characterized by specific and identifiable moral activities. For proof of this hypothesis or even suggestions of how it might be tested, we look in vain. Zink "proves" his case by assertion, and thus his proof cannot compel assent.

If Zink is only a partially helpful guide, the social scientists have been no more helpful. One scans *Sociological Abstracts* and *Psychological Abstracts* in vain for definitive studies.[29] Robert E. Lane's *The Liberties of Wit: Humanism, Criticism, and the Civic Mind* (1961) appears at first to be promising because the author has expertise in political science, sociology, and literary criticism. His account of the problem and the ineffectual response of most critics to it is admirably lucid.

> What effects does [literature] have on various readers and types of readers—the best as well as the average? We have asked for theory, organization, verification. Now we need the fruits of such study, for in order to talk seriously about the beneficial values of literary study, we should know what the effects are first. There are many books on aesthetics with theories on this matter, but on examination it turns out that they are based upon four kinds of evidence: the introspection of the author into the qualities of his own experience, the author's empathic sense of how this experience might or should affect others (particularly others like himself), the report of other authors on these two matters, and the report of poets on how they and others feel about poetry. This is not negligible; the report of a sensitive man on his own experience is valuable and must be incorporated in any analysis as a useful piece of evidence. But it suffers from the usual deficiencies of introspection, selective perception, idiosyncratic notation, and lack of comparability of findings, inaccessibility of the unconscious, rationalization. Moreover it is structured in the terminol-

ogy of an outdated, usually "home made" psychology which . . . today carries limited conviction. On the other hand, a more or less systematic search through the recent encyclopedias, anthologies, handbooks, and bibliographies of sociology, social psychology, anthropology, and psychiatry does not reveal much useful material in assessing the value of literature to the individual.[30]

But the analysis of the problem is more astute than the response to it. Lane confesses that he simply does not know whether "the study of literature affects the conscience, the morality, the sensitivity of some code of 'right' and 'wrong.'" And so he contents himself with a recital of the received ideas: literature gives one a sense to purpose or mission, helps one achieve an identity, ensures a sense of tradition, and so on. These are important values, and it is quite possible that literature does accomplish some or all of them. But unless these assertions are properly investigated and verified, modern apologists can hardly continue to claim them when pressed to defend literary preferences or assertions about the moral effects of particular works. Such criticism as Alfred Harbage's, for example, would be more convincing if Harbage's claims about Shakespeare's "moral artistry" were supported by something other than metaphor. "Shakespeare is a dramatic artist, and the relation of dramatic art to the moral nature of man is about that of wind to the surface of water. It keeps the surface agitated, spanking it into sunny little ripples or driving it into powerful surges, but it does not trouble the depths. Dramatic art neither raises nor lowers the level, and the business of the dramatic artist is to know the height of the surface upon which he works."[31]

Harbage's conception of Shakespeare's moral artistry differs sharply from Johnson's. It is logically impossible for the premises of both critics to be valid: Johnson certainly would not be justified, according to Harbage's principle, in objecting to Shakespeare's moral lapses since the dramatic artist "does not trouble the depths." But Harbage, like Johnson before him, holds his claims to be self-evident. William Righter notes that rigorous logic is seldom a feature of literary criticism and that in practical criticism there is actually very little demand for a full justification of any judgement, and in fact it is unclear what such a "full" justification could be. There is normally an agreed area of critical dispute, the lines of argument are understood, and as soon as the particular issue has been explored and the points of view towards it clarified, the discussion does not go much further. One is seldom asked to make points of a very general and inclusive nature, say, to show that James really is a great, good or plausible novelist.[32]

Or that Shakespeare "does not trouble the depths" or that Restoration comedy is moral.

To the extent that literary criticism is a type of rational discourse concerned with making defensible propositions ("Congreve *really is* a great dramatist") about literary works or authors, some attempt at a "full justification" is germane, especially when the issue is as fundamental to aesthetics and, more broadly, to traditional assumptions about the humanities as this one. Relativists would not dream of a full justification. Frederick Pottle's relativism, which he champions as a critical principle, is insufficient because it renders all critical judgments solipsistic: one can speak meaningfully of and describe accurately only one's own responses. No reader's judgment of Restoration comedy is more "right" than another's. "All original criticism is subjective, being a report of the impact of the work upon the critic's sensibility; all criticism is relative to the critic's sensibility; and the question as to a 'right' sensibility does not arise."[33] But surely the question of a "right judgment" does arise unless one has complete confidence at all times in one's judgment, even in a first impression. Pottle might reply that all readings are right but some are more right. But even if Pottle is unconcerned with "right judgment" or a "full justification" of a position, other modern critics have looked closely at the literary enactment of moral values and thus merit brief attention.

Sheldon Sacks's *Fiction and the Shape of Belief* (1964) is an impressive attempt to learn how novelists, particularly Fielding, articulate their moral beliefs. After establishing the categories of satire, apologue, and novel, Sacks analyzes the rhetorical techniques by which novelists control our response to and evaluation of the action and characters. Sacks asks a difficult question— "What must the author of this novel have believed to have evaluated as he did such characters?"[34]—and then provides a methodology for answering it. In essence, his approach requires very close stylistic analysis and sensitivity to the presence and function of various classes of characters.[35] He concludes that "a good novelist embodies his beliefs and opinions in such a way that a particularized ethical effect is an assured consequence of his whole *novel*" (p. 254). Sacks's study is learned and helpful and may provide a paradigm for working with the ethical effects of fiction, but its applicability to moral evaluation of other genres has not been tested.

Working specifically with the lyric poem but more generally with the problem of "the relation between the patterns [the critic] objectively finds in the text and a reader's subjective experience of the text,"[36] Norman N. Holland returns in *The Dynamics of Literary Response* to many of the assumptions and arguments of *The First Modern Comedies*. Puzzled that "anyone in the last third of the twentieth century" should be concerned about moral evaluation of literature,[37] Holland gets down to "the real business of criticism" as he understands it. His ambition is to scrutinize psychoanalytically his own response to works of literature. He contends that literature transforms nuclear fantasies "toward meaningfulness and thereby allows them to elude the censoring part of our minds and achieve an oblique expression and gratification" (p. 310). After sharing with the reader the contours of his responses to works, Holland asks whether literature provides anything except the gratification of ego-mastery. Is there moral instruction, or, in other words, is it sensible to ask whether literature significantly alters human behavior? His answer is equivocal. "[Literature] seems to have two, in a way opposite possibilities for moral effect. First, literature may reinforce or counter the defenses and adaptations our culture builds into us. Second, literature lets us experience those and other values in a more open, 'as if' way. . . . Yet, given the firmness of cultural structure and individual character, it is very hard to see how the effects of literature can be more than small, local, and transient" (p. 340).

Holland does not really say that literature, whether a lyric poem or a Restoration comedy, has a calculable or predictable moral effect. It *may*, but it is unlikely, since potential readers are acculturated before they are literate, and besides, character is predominantly formed before the age of five, long before anyone might read, say, *The London Cuckolds*. Holland seems to deny the "utile" half of the Horatian equation, but he hedges. In another passage he is somewhat more explicit. "In short, a free literature seems not so much to teach for or against a given set of cultural values as to keep open, at least for the time of reading, the possibility of change. Like the adolescent, we try on roles. . . . The moral effect of literature, then, is to create not long-term change in itself, but a possibility of change" (pp. 337, 338). While not really granting that Restoration comedy may effect change, Holland distinguishes between causing a change and allowing the possibility of change.

What might Holland say about Restoration comedy if he used the psychoanalytical model that he uses on lyric poetry? He might say that the plays provide lively entertainment and allow the readers to experience vicarious liberation from workaday restraints. Readers could try on various roles, keeping open the possibility of change in their lives. But would readers be more likely to try on the role, say, of Harcourt than of Horner? Holland would probably say that it is an interesting possibility. Whether it would be desirable for readers to adopt Horner's values, if not his tactics, would be a wholly different kind of question, one unrelated to the critic's proper purview because it involves ethical judgment and evaluation. Neither of these is fashionable, as he said earlier, "in the last third of the twentieth century," so he might dismiss the question as alien to the critic's responsibility. The determination of what effects, if any, Restoration comedy tends to promote and the evaluation of those effects by an external ethical standard involves a discipline and a methodology foreign to his own approach ("As with most psycho-

The Critics' Dilemma

analytic research, we must work from a case history, and in this situation, the case is me" [p. xiv]).

Clearly, Holland values "the possibility of change" as an important component of the "right sensibility," but such a touchstone is multivalent. If one understands the phrase as a circumlocution for "tolerance," the difficulty is still not resolved. One cannot simply be tolerant; one must be tolerant *of*. And there the ethical question erupts once more. To rely on "experience" or "the possibility of change" or "enlargement of sympathy" as moral touchstones is to replace Johnson's Procrustes with Holland's Proteus: and it is no more certain that literature keeps open the possibility of change than that it "instructs," as Johnson understood moral instruction through literature.

When a modern critic asserts that Restoration comedy is moral, what prompts him to make that kind of judgment? There are several possible explanations. First, the critic is automatically acknowledging a particular kind of value in the work. He may perceive in the comedy a vision of human life harmonious with his own; in short, the proper characters are rewarded and punished. The critic is thus making an ethical judgment about the content, structure, or conduct of the comedy. Or the critic may argue that the comedy is moral because it provides a full and rich aesthetic experience, and any aesthetic object capable of providing this kind of experience is moral. This critic would seek to avoid the invidious distinction between form and content that the first critic made by regarding the *richness* of the experience as the sole criterion of value. And a third critic might synthesize the prior approaches by praising the fullness of the aesthetic experience as well as endorsing the moral vision, which complements, of course, his own. In these positions, the key word is *experience*.

Many modern critics outside the great tradition have tried to chart the dimensions of the aesthetic *experience* itself. The task is particularly inviting to critics of a scientific disposition, for it demands that the scientist investigate the topography of the human spirit by mapping its peculiarities as well as its common features. Perhaps the most graphic example is I. A. Richards's famous neurological diagram of how a poem is read.[38] John Dewey spends many pages discussing how one has an experience,[39] ultimately trying to distinguish the aesthetic experience from other types. Philip Rahv deals rather more broadly with Americans' seemingly unappeasable appetite for experience in "The Cult of Experience in American Writing."[40] Indeed, one could say that for much of modern aesthetics and culture, "experience" functions like "nature" in Pope's *Essay on Criticism*: "At once the *Source*, and *End*, and *Test* of *Art*" (l. 73). But the difference between "experience" and "nature" as the basis of literary evaluation and other moral judgments is crucial: notwithstanding Lovejoy's discriminations among the meanings of "nature," the word had a normative function for its age that "experience" lacks for ours. When a critic waxes about the "fullness" or "complexity" or "coherence" of an aesthetic experience—these are common abstractions frequently used to characterize "experience"—he is suggesting something about the impact of the work. Whether the experience has anything more than an impact is not usually investigated.

One's capacity to have an aesthetic experience is affected by numerous factors, none discussed comfortably by critics in an egalitarian society. The eighteenth century was not as squeamish on this or other matters: in Augustan England, one recalls, butchers were barred from serving on juries because it was believed that their work had debased their sensibilities. Shaftesbury, after all, had confidently assumed almost a causal relationship between taste and morality. What was inherently distasteful was likely to be morally debilitating. But as William Righter suggests in *Logic and Criticism,* "background, intelligence, education, and taste inevitably impose themselves on all of our reactions to literature, including preference, choice and judgment."[41] Since one assumes that the capacity to have an "aesthetic experience" is a desideratum of the civilized and literate reader, one might also wonder about the long-term consequences of enjoying aesthetic experiences.

Modern literary critics, even though they often make moral judgments of literary works, seldom consider this question. If

The Critics' Dilemma

they do not rely on the authority of the great tradition to sanction their view, then they may rely on "experience" as a touchstone of value and thereby hope to avoid making explicit ethical judgments about literature.[42] Clearly, the second approach begs the question as surely as the critics in the great tradition had done. The larger problem of art and morality is passed over.

While I have suggested at several points the relevance of this discussion to the *moralisé* tradition, it will be helpful now to place the issue in a fuller context. We have seen that the morality of Restoration comedy has been defended on vastly different grounds during the past three centuries. The *réaliste* critics may differ considerably in their perception of the moral *content* of the plays, but they agree that this content is moral by whatever standards they adopt. An implicit part of their argument is that the representation of "moral" content encourages the kind of moral values or social conduct enacted by the plays. The *artificielle* critics are not concerned whether the content is moral; the comedies achieve a moral effect by temporarily anesthetizing the sober and censorious part of the reader's sensibility. Thus, the apologists reach the same general conclusion by substantially different paths. All, however, make an ethical judgment of the kind of experience afforded by Restoration comedy.

Because of the focus on the literary experience, several problems arise. When one makes an ethical judgment of a literary work, how much emphasis can be given the moral judgment without erecting discrete categories of value, one for the form (of particular interest to the *artificielle* critics) and one for the content (of particular interest to the *réaliste* critics)? Is not this rather like the critical practice of the *Gentleman's Magazine,* which ranked dramatists by their genius, judgment, learning, and versification?[43] If a critic finds such a dichotomy as form and content theoretically unsound but still feels obliged to make a moral judgment of the work (as most critics have done), how far does the use of moral criteria "even if in an undogmatic way [illuminate] the works of art . . . or how far [does it distort them]?"[44] Does a moral judgment of a work inevitably lead away from the work and focus on ethics? In other words, does literature become something other than itself when one focuses on moral philosophy? If this kind of criticism leads eventually to philosophy, why not start there and eliminate the circuitous enterprise of literary scholarship and criticism?

The question of moral effects has been made so unmanageable because critics have been reluctant to answer adequately or consider fully these and other questions related more specifically to dramatic literature. 1) If critics are to base their criticism on the effects they imagine the work to have on an audience, do they not need to demonstrate the existence of those effects and develop ways to measure them? 2) Is it reasonable to assume that the concept of audience is less an abstraction than the concept of "the critic"? That is, if the critic speaks of the moral effects of a work on an audience, does he not need to specify which audience and consider the varieties of responses likely within that audience? 3) Do different genres virtually by definition arouse different kinds of effects? That is, do different types of literature work on different aesthetic principles and invite different degrees of involvement? For example, does farce "work" in the same way as satiric comedy? Is it reasonable to expect that a lyric poem and an historical novel and a court masque in which one is an actor will affect one in the same way? Without adequate answers to these questions, critics who argue about the moral effects of Restoration comedy proceed from an uncertain logical position.

Many of the modern critics who make a "moral" claim about Restoration comedy, whether incidentally in practical criticism or explicitly in a fuller apology for literature, are part of a lengthy critical tradition that has defended literature for its supposed moral utility. While secular critics tend not to discuss the relative merits of various moral codes—the ones that seem to be embedded in the plays, the critics' own values, the values of the critics' age, and so on—all seem inevitably drawn toward the ethical response to and evaluation of Restoration comedy.

The importance of considering such a question is obvious, for the critics touch on a cardinal belief of humanists for many centuries, namely, that literature is in some way instructive and en-

The Critics' Dilemma

nobling. Though critics are loath to engage in what Righter calls a "full justification" of their position, critics in the *moralisé* tradition have been persistently involved in a controversy whose ultimate universe of discourse is ethics and whose ultimate concern is with the nature of the good life. Critics who claim that they are not "moral" critics (e.g., Holland) or who will defer discussion of the moral issues (e.g., Knights) do not avoid the problem dealt with more forthrightly by critics who consciously evaluate their literary responses by explicit ethical standards; such critics merely rely on their own particular version of morality as the norm.

If one cannot help but engage in a moral response to the comedies, one still can choose to be explicit rather than vague, forthright rather than disingenuous, about the relation of one's "profoundest ethical sensibility," in Leavis's words, to Restoration comedy. Such candor and self-knowledge encourage criticism *engagé* rather than the "anesthetic criticism"[45] that Frederick Crews deplores and that Edmund Wilson attacks as one of the "fruits" of the MLA.[46] What may emerge from skillfully presented *moralisé* criticism is discourse in which ideas are once more taken seriously and evaluated critically and in which rational debate is used to analyze the good, the true, and the beautiful. Those matters have not been considered directly by professional critics for a long time, and they are worthy of their attention.

Regardless of the complex problems that attend the moral evaluation of literature, the success of which depending as in other types of criticism on one's sensitivity, intelligence, and sophistication,[47] the question central to this study remains unanswered. What kind or kinds of moral effects does a Restoration comedy have? It is insufficient to answer the question by assuming that because art may have certain effects, the comedy, too, will have certain moral effects. Furthermore, it is an unanswered question whether one could use the methods of the social sciences to discover changes in the reader solely attributable to literature. No research thus far supports that claim. The alternative is to look closely at individual works so that their distinctive moral vision can be discerned. One cannot help but view art through the lenses of one's own moral orientation: there is no "objective" criticism of a literary text. But one can acknowledge one's assumptions and values and proceed to examine the elements of plot, character, language, genre, and dramatic structure by which dramatists enact meaning and embody their view of human life. To approach such comedies as *The London Cuckolds* and *The Country Wife* with these intentions is to realize that their moral visions are not easily discerned, and to discuss them at all requires careful consideration of the dramatists' techniques and the dramatic traditions that shape late seventeenth-century literature.

5

"Deep-breathing sex" and Critical Practice

> Professor Knight praised the "clarity and lack of grain" in the photography and said [*Deep Throat*] was not given to "deep-breathing sex." "Didn't you hear the female in the opening scene breathe deeply?" Judge Tyler asked severely. Professor Knight said he had been speaking metaphorically. (*New York Times*, 21 December 1972, p. 40)
>
> *Hamlet.* Do you see yonder cloud that's almost in shape of a camel?
> *Polonius.* By the mass, and 'tis like a camel indeed.
> *Hamlet.* Methinks it is like a weasel.
> *Polonius.* It is backed like a weasel.
> *Hamlet.* Or like a whale?
> *Polonius.* Very like a whale. (III.ii)

Like all imaginative literature, Restoration comedies provoke the critic to examine not only his assumptions about life but the adequacy of his perception of and his response to the text. Just as Polonius was able to "see" the protean shapes before Hamlet's eyes, the modern reader of Restoration comedies, for example, one who is familiar with the criticism in which *The Country Wife* has been found either "moral" or "immoral," may find that Wycherley's comedy has no permanent shape or meaning, susceptible instead to quite contradictory interpretations. Quite aside from Wycherley's intentions or his claims about his intentions, what moral vision is in fact enacted in the comedy? What can be said about Edward Ravenscroft's *The London Cuckolds* (1681), a comedy that enjoyed enormous popularity for nearly a century but is characterized by Nicoll as "flagrant," with a "perfectly immoral plot, descending, because of its workmanship, to utter vulgarity."[1] Steele and Cibber thought it contemptible, David Garrick ceased to present it on Lord Mayor's Day after 1751, James Sutherland calls it "the old pagan comedy of sex, the worship of Dionysius in seventeenth-century London,"[2] and Robert D. Hume regards it as "blithely indecent."[3] To use the language of Judge Tyler and Professor Knight, how metaphorical is the deep-breathing sex in these works?

To discover the moral vision of a Restoration comedy is much more challenging than to summarize its plot and analyze its characters, though these are necessary steps. By "moral vision" I refer to the moral values that are dominant in a work, the vision of human life and of human relationships that every work of imaginative literature enacts in its distinctive way, whether a masque by Ben Jonson or a comedy by Samuel Beckett. To claim that a Restoration comedy embodies a distinctive moral vision is not to claim, however, that it necessarily affects the values or behavior of its audience, for it is by no means clear that works of literature, singly or collectively, tend to cause particular changes or to affect their audience in predictable or easily measured ways.[4]

At stake is the fundamental issue of how we perceive a work of literature. Harriet Hawkins properly stresses that the critic's first task is to see and describe what is present in the text without imposing on it extraneous qualities peculiar to himself or his age.[5] While perception must precede judgment, the very act of perceiving a comedy, of participating in its imagined universe, immediately engages a reader's sympathy and judgment, forcing the reader to consider the nature of his response to the characters and the work. One of the initial perceptual and judgmental decisions that the reader makes is how literally or metaphorically he should regard the work: that is, when is "deep-breathing sex" not deep-breathing sex but something else, something symbolic or allegorical?[6]

Critical Practice

Chaucer's "Merchant's Tale," the story of a *senex amans* cuckolded by his youthful wife, could serve as an analogue of the plots in many seventeenth-century comedies, from Moliere's *L'Ecole des femmes* to Southerne's *The Wives Excuse: or, Cuckolds Make Themselves*. The story of January and May is not so much a story of adultery as an anatomy of cupidity, of January's inordinate desire to possess a wife without regard for her wishes or for the proper grounds of matrimony. Chaucer's graphic account of the nuptial bed is no ethereal epithalamion.

> *Thus laboureth he til that the day gan dawe;*
> *And thanne he taketh a sop in fyn clarree,*
> *And upright in his bed thanne sitteth he,*
> *And after that he sang ful loude and cleere,*
> *And kiste his wyf, and made wantown cheere.*
> *He was as coltissh, ful of ragereye,*
> *And ful of jargon as a flekked pye.*
> *The slakke skyn about his nekke shaketh,*
> *Whil that he sang, so chaunteth he and craketh.*
> *But God woot what that May thoughte in hir herte,*
> *Whan she hym saugh up sittynge in his sherte,*
> *In his nyghte-cappe, and with his nekke lene;*
> *She preyseth nat his pleyyng worth a bene.*[7]

D. W. Robertson, Jr., and other historical critics have provided modern readers with detailed knowledge of the richly symbolic language familiar to Chaucer and his audience, sensitizing them to the reverberations of Chaucer's language, his particular use of iconic and symbolic references (the characters' names, the symbolism of the pear tree, and so on) through which a moral vision is encoded at more than the literal level of the narrative. Chaucer's frequent use of cuckoldry in *The Canterbury Tales*, far from endorsing adultery as a moral norm, discloses a moral universe where cuckoldry is inflicted as deserved punishment, where sins of the flesh are punished in kind. This approach to the meaning of "The Merchant's Tale" could almost serve as an introduction to the problems of perceiving and interpreting *The London Cuckolds* and *The Country Wife*.

Since Ravenscroft's works are unfamiliar to modern readers—

no modern text of *The London Cuckolds* is readily available[8]—I will provide a detailed summary of plot and character before considering its moral vision. In its simplest terms, the plot repeats a single action three times with only slight variation: the horning of three aged cits, Wiseacre, Doodle, and Dashwell. The action is complicated partly by the inventiveness of three young wits (Townly, Ramble, and Loveday) but more significantly by the old men's obdurate pride in their imagined immunity to horns. Each aged husband claims to have found the only way to preserve his wife's fidelity and hence his own honor. Wiseacre insists that the only safeguard is his wife's ignorance.

> That I might be sure not to be troubled with a witty wife, I made choice of a Girle of four years of age, one that had no signs of a pregnant wit, her father and mother were none of the wisest; they dying, left this child to the care of her Aunt, a good honest decay'd Gentlewoman, but a little soft too; her portion they recommended to my hand, to be improv'd for her use; I plac'd the Aunt and child in the Countrey, at a lone house, instructed her to breed her up in all honesty and simplicity imaginable; never to let her play amongst Boyes or Girles, or have any conversation with any body but her self; and now being bred to my own humour, and moulded to my turn, I am going to reap the fruits of my long care and trouble, for this is she I design for my wife. (P. 2)

He has brought up a "fool" and vows to keep her so, locked in the bonds of matrimony. Ironically, Doodle mentions to him that even schoolgirls are corruptible: he had recently seen two *young* girls reading "the beastly, bawdy translated book called the Schoole of Women" (p. 2), Molière's comedy (1662) in which Arnolphe tries to avoid cuckoldom by having Agnes, supposedly a peasant's daughter, reared in rural simplicity so that she will learn no artful deceptions. Of course he fails, for Horace, a young wit, eventually rescues and marries her. The lesson is lost on both men, alas.

Doodle intends to avoid the horns by the opposite tactic and has married a witty wife. "If my wife was a fool, I should always suspect her a whore, for 'tis want of wit that makes 'em believe the flatteries of men; she that has sense will discern their traps and snares and avoid 'em: I tell you, Mr. Alderman, a woman without sense, is like a castle without souldiers, to be taken at every assault" (p. 3). Arabella, his wife of six months, will best defend *his* honor by frequenting the theatre and by socializing among the beau monde.

Dashwell rejects both friends' strategies. "Then let me tell you for both your comforts," he confides, "a wife that has wit will outwit her husband, and she that has no wit will be out witted by others beside her husband, and so 'tis an equal lay, which makes the husband a Cuckold first or oftenest" (p. 4). He has solved his problem by marrying a religious woman who "prays and goest often to Church" (p. 4). To his colleagues' jibes that such women are brazen hypocrites, summoned to assignations by the tolling of every church bell, Dashwell smugly affirms that he alone is secure.

A second trio, the gallants, complicates the plot. Ned Ramble and Frank Townly, paralleling the aldermen's discussion of how to keep a wife, discuss how to gain a mistress. Ramble bemoans his bad luck in courtship, describing how he has failed thus far to win the favor of Eugenia, who had married Dashwell against her will. Unfortunately for Ramble, he has arranged a tryst with both Eugenia and Arabella that night. As Act I ends, Townly curses Ramble for refusing to share his good fortune.

This curse is realized early in Act II, for Valentine Loveday, Eugenia's suitor before her forced marriage, calls on her while disguised as a servant seeking employment. After being rushed off to bed, he observes the banquet that Eugenia has prepared for Ramble. When Dashwell suddenly returns home to impress Doodle with Eugenia's piety, he finds her at prayer. Nevertheless, he insists on displaying his faithful wife to his friend. Not realizing that Eugenia has more than one man hidden in her room, Dashwell is surprised to find Loveday in residence. Claiming to be a scholar expelled from Oxford for conjuring, Loveday demonstrates his finesse in the black arts by producing not only a fine meal for Dashwell and Doodle (i.e., the banquet prepared for Eugenia and Ramble) but his "familiar" in human shape, Ned Ramble.

In the next scene Ramble sees Peggy, Wiseacre's country wife, and is enraptured. Fearful of losing Peggy to this rake, Wiseacre and Peggy disappear along a darkened street. When Townly spies Ramble searching for Peggy, he hides in the dark and answers Jane, Eugenia's servant, when she calls for Ramble. Townly then accompanies her to Eugenia's bedroom where Dashwell is sleeping, literally and symbolically. Seeing Townly embrace Eugenia as he departs, Ramble attacks both of them. Jane and Eugenia, fearing that Dashwell has discovered their ruse, run back to their rooms.

As the third act begins, Arabella is worried that she may have confused Ramble with Townly. Thus, when Ramble returns, she coldly resists him for a few moments, yielding only when he grows eloquent:

> Come, Madam, act not against your Conscience, I know how matters go; you are a fine, a young, brisk, handsome Lady, and have a dull dronish Husband without a sting, I am a young active fellow fit for imployment, and 'ygad I know your wants, and for once will throw my self upon you, therefore come, Madam, come, your night-dress becomes you so well, and you look so very tempting—I can hardly forbear you a minute longer. (P. 27)

Doodle's sudden return interrupts the results of Ramble's rhetoric, sending Ramble into hiding and provoking Arabella's witty badinage with her slow-witted husband. After Doodle finally falls asleep, Engine, Arabella's servant, is to take Arabella's place beside him so that Arabella can enjoy Ramble's company. But Roger, Ramble's faithful servant, fears for Ramble's safety when he sees Doodle's return. Crying fire to help his master escape, Roger succeeds only in interrupting the romance.

After chastising Roger for his untimely inventiveness, Ramble attempts to reenter Doodle's house through a cellar window but becomes stuck halfway through. Engine's laughter awakens a neighbor, who empties a chamberpot onto Ramble just after a linkboy had singed his face. Finally, when two chimney sweepers are about to "flip a point" in his face, he cries out that he is a gentleman. They consider him a thief and steal his hat, sword, and periwig before blackening his face. This commotion rouses the watchman, who arrests Ramble and awakens Doodle, who vigilantly fires his fowling piece into the empty window and then listens credulously to Ramble's canard. His honor as a gallant blackened like his face, Ramble wanders home.

His hopes revive, however, when he receives a billet-doux from Eugenia at the beginning of the fourth act. While Eugenia and Jane await Ramble a third time, Loveday discovers them and reveals himself as Eugenia's former lover. He explains to Eugenia how their parents had quashed their love by telling each that the other was dead. Her heart stirred once more, Eugenia tells Jane to cancel her tryst with Ramble. Dashwell's unexpected return, however, requires that Loveday hide in her bed. After Dashwell leaves, Ramble arrives to claim his due, but Dashwell's sudden appearance sends Ramble into hiding in Eugenia's bedchamber. This time, though, Ramble plays a bolder part than in the second act, where Loveday had "conjured" him away. Ramble now claims to be searching for a man who had conjured up a Devil in his shape. Eugenia and Jane confess to Dashwell that they hid this conjuror in Eugenia's bedchamber to protect him. Despondent and frustrated, Ramble departs once more, for Dashwell seems to have returned for the evening. Dashwell's friends, Wiseacre and Doodle, have left him to attend to a ship newly come into port. Neither is concerned about his wife's fidelity: Wiseacre has left Peggy on their wedding night with instructions that she is to wear armor and guard his nightcap until his return; Doodle has placed a linguistic handcuff on his witty wife, allowing her to say nothing except no to any other man's questions.

As the last act begins, the three gallants prepare for their last assault on the defenses erected by the three old men. Arabella discovers that she can conduct a successful intrigue with Townly (pp. 40–41) despite her monosyllabic responses. Having seen Peggy walking in armor, Ramble is anxious to continue her education in the duties of a wife. Loveday decides to thwart Dashwell once more by arranging to thrash him. Eugenia agrees to tell Dashwell about Loveday's entreaties and persuades Dashwell to beat the arrant suitor.

As Wiseacre and Doodle return from the docks, each stresses his confidence that *his* domestic strategy is the only means to escape cuckoldry. Moreover, each believes the other to have been duped by an unfaithful wife. As Doodle looks for a glove he has dropped, Ramble drops down on him from Peggy's balcony and beats him. At once Doodle suspects that his assailant has been dabbling with Peggy and is not assaulting him but escaping from her balcony. When Wiseacre hears that Peggy has gone to bed despite her orders and has learned a "duty" more invigorating than the regimen he had prescribed, he is livid but still unconvinced that he has been cozened. Doodle's security does not last much longer. Encountering a high-spirited Townly, Wiseacre asks why he is so amused. Townly replies that he has found a woman who can only say no. Wiseacre kindly volunteers to show Townly his mistress's identity, so they return to Doodle's house. As Townly begins to tell his story again—to Arabella's horror—Arabella drops her ring into his glass of sack. Despite this signal, he recounts in graphic detail his experience, terrifying Arabella, worrying Doodle, and pleasing Wiseacre. But Townly abruptly concludes that his experience was only a dream, which is of no solace to Doodle but relief to Arabella and confirmation to Wiseacre. Soon after, Dashwell tells his friends to end their debate on the merits of a witty or foolish wife: if they want to see a zealous wife, they should see Eugenia.

Proud that he has been told of Loveday's impropriety, Dashwell waits confidently in the garden for him. Loveday enters, loudly declares his true devotion to Eugenia, and then "caresses" Dashwell with his whip. Eugenia, in mock outrage, says she will have Loveday beaten, first for tempting her and then for beating her beloved spouse. Despite the laughter of Doodle and Wiseacre, Dashwell maintains that Loveday meant no harm and in fact was "testing" Eugenia for her own good. Despite his colleagues' speculations on the true nature and probable results of the test, Dashwell is as adamant as the others: "I would not yet change my Wife for her that a man leapt from her Window, nor for the Lady *No*, of whom that Gentleman Dream'd such a fine Dream there, ha, ha, ha" (p. 58).

In the final scene, the Aunt, a watchman, and Ramble encounter Doodle, who swears that it was Ramble who had jumped from the balcony. Swearing that Ramble stole nothing visible, Peggy asks only that her tutor continue his teaching. Loveday reveals his identity to Dashwell, who is greatly alarmed by the reappearance of Eugenia's former suitor. Doodle's bravado in claiming once again his primacy at regulating his wife's sexual behavior is answered with a resounding no.

The London Cuckolds provides an excellent instance of the difficulties that beset a critic interested in the moral vision of Restoration comedies. How does one respond to the frantic shuffling from bedchamber to balcony, the manic assignations, the uncertain concealment and furtive disclosure of identity and motive? Certainly there is ample deep-breathing: the wives must conceal lovers, sometimes more than one simultaneously, in their bedrooms; the lovers risk chamberpots and excrement as they tunnel into assignations; husbands are affronted by their colleagues' blindness but cannot see their own myopia. The subject of the play would appear to be little more than the varieties of offensive and defensive maneuvers in sexual warfare. But the critic who looks at more than the literal level of the play may certainly speculate whether the comedy can be "moralized," read in such a way that the cuckolding, say, serves as an instrument of poetic justice and thus ensures a traditional moral vision. If that is the case, then is the play primarily about cuckolding? In short, what are the "moral facts" about this "notorious piece" and its "perfectly immoral plot"?

The plot of *The London Cuckolds* focuses exclusively on the cuckolding of three aged citizens, which would seem to place it in the tradition of what Robert D. Hume calls "sex comedy," a type of comic drama popularized by Durfey's *A Fond Husband* (1677) and widely imitated throughout the 1670s and 1680s. But one should ask what this play says about cuckolding, for its tone clearly differs from that of Southerne's bitter satire *The Wives Ex-*

cuse: or, Cuckolds Make Themselves or Dryden's *Marriage-à-la-Mode*, both of which deal prominently with sexual relations. If the play is satiric, then its objects of satire and an ethical framework by which its satiric butts are to be judged should be identifiable. But what is satirized in the play? One could argue that lust, hypocrisy, jealousy, or pride is ridiculed, but this means that each trio of characters—the old men, the young men, and the young wives—is culpable, for Ravenscroft ensures that each trio is "punished" in some way. Each of the cits is exposed to his friends' ridicule; the two "experienced" wives constantly risk exposure and ridicule; and Ramble shoulders the brunt of his peers' punishment, being exposed to ridicule on numerous occasions. In short, while it is clear that the husbands are the central figures of ridicule, the wives and the witwouds also have their illusions punctured and their plans disrupted, making them look absurd. Who or what is satirized?

With no romantic plot or idealized lovers to provide a counterpoint to the gallants' intrigues, the play combines two common plot formulas, the gulling of the pretentious, and cuckolding. Ravenscroft fuses the gulling and cuckolding plots since the object of both plots—the cuckolding of a *senex amans*—is the same. In *The London Cuckolds*, sex is like gold in *The Alchemist*, something both concrete and symbolic in its galvanizing effect on and hypnotic allure to those who covet it. But unlike Jonson's satiric comedy, the tone remains light: Ravenscroft's characters are not anatomized under the corrective lens of satire, which reveals their underlying crudity or viciousness. His characters are one-dimensional and static. What is base is immediately shown to be base, and the characters neither improve nor degenerate as a result of interaction with other characters.

But does not the farcical tone of *The London Cuckolds* obviate such serious criticism? The risqué dialogue, the obscene puns, the disguises and mistaken identities, the slapstick (e.g., Ramble's entrapment in a window, the conjuring scene, the guarding of the nightcap, physical assaults on characters, and so on), and the hide-and-seek bedroom antics make this work farcical rather than satirical. Hume regards farce as the "least serious" of the eight types of Restoration comedy (p. 72) but does not explore the aesthetic implications of this classification. That is, does classifying a comedy as farce eliminate traditional considerations of theme, meaning, and vision?

In one sense the comedy touches on themes more seriously amplified in other comedies of the period (e.g., the misery of enforced marriage), but these motifs are merely given lip service by the characters and are not developed dramatically into major themes. For example, Ramble reports that "by the Inducement of her Parents [Eugenia] Married [Dashwell] against her inclinations, and now nauseating her Husband's bed, rises every Morning by Five or Six with a pretence to hear Lectures and Sermons, and loathing his Company at home, pretends all day to be at Prayers" (p. 8). But Ravenscroft does not exploit Eugenia's situation: to do so would result in quite another kind of comedy. Eugenia's motives for marriage provide a hint for her interest in lovers, not an analysis of a social system in which a major purpose of some marriages was to consolidate or acquire estates and in which other grounds for matrimony were often ignored. Ravenscroft exploits the comic potential of sexual escapades—the dramatic tension of concealing two lovers from a husband in the same bedroom—and titillates his audience without arguing that relationships based on love are superior to those based on economic or erotic interests. The erotic scenes compel interest because of their likelihood of failure: surely Dashwell will discover one or more of Arabella's lovers during one of his impromptu returns home, and the ensuing comic explosion of accusation and prevarication should provide lively entertainment.

Furthermore, Ravenscroft does not exploit contemporary social or political tensions, another way to invest the comedy with "serious" meaning and to darken its tone. To be sure, the Whigs in *The London Cuckolds* are pompous fools, ignoring their wives on wedding nights, marrying "innocents" who have been reared in ignorance of the world, and deceiving themselves about their wives' fidelity. But to compare this play to Crowne's *City Politiques* (1682), which depicts the cuckolding of Whigs as just payment for their machinations in the Popish Plot, is to realize how apolitical Ravenscroft is. Tensions between Cavaliers and Puritans, Tories and Whigs, and courtiers and merchants are simply undeveloped, eclipsed by the conflict between the young and the old, a division that cuts across or transcends social, economic, political, or religious commitments. Incipient political or social themes are overshadowed by the vaudeville atmosphere. Moreover, if the play might be thought to derogate Whigs, then the Whigs who comprise an increasingly important part of the audience from 1660 to 1710 seem not to have been offended.[9] The play was a fixture of Lord Mayor's Day pageantry until 1751, when David Garrick removed it from his repertoire for aesthetic, not political, reasons: its ribald spirit, which complemented the festive spirit of the oratory, fireworks, and carousing that marked Lord Mayor's Days for five centuries, simply was incompatible with the theatrical tastes of mid-eighteenth-century London. Far from giving offense for political reasons, the play was performed frequently in London for nearly seventy-five years.

Indeed, it can be argued that in farce the image of life is so patently oversimplified, the characterization so thin, the plot so farfetched, that an audience expecting the intellectual challenge and moral edification of a Jonson or a Molière is bound to be disappointed. Themes can undoubtedly be identified in *The London Cuckolds,* just as some television cartoons popular today can be shown to echo the myth of Sisyphus (how many times can a cat or coyote or obtuse hunter stalk unsuccessfully a mouse, roadrunner, or rabbit?). To perceive farce as though it were satiric comedy raises expectations that the play cannot satisfy. The contempt of late seventeenth-century dramatists for farce is not based solely on their resentment of its immediate success with contemporary audiences. In the year-to-year competition between barely solvent theatrical companies, a successful innovation at one theatre was quickly imitated by the other companies.[10] Another basis for contempt is the dramatists' awareness that farce is comedy stripped of its ethical base, its moral assumptions, and its didactic purpose. Farce expropriates the language and some of the structural devices and character types of

Critical Practice

comedy, but in farce meaning does not exfoliate from the clash of characters and the values they represent. Farce arouses laughter but does not direct it beyond the jibe or spectacle of the moment: it ridicules but only the most obvious foibles or flaws. Farce also complicates the critic's task, for the Restoration stage offers not only farces and farcical afterpieces but, most troublesome to analyze, "serious" comedies that include elements of farce. It is tempting for a critic uncomfortable with the moral vision, say, of *The London Cuckolds* or *The Country Wife* to call it a "farce," thereby excusing the work from further analysis. Robert D. Hume takes this approach in his analysis of Wycherley's comedy, a play that illustrates his working definition of "sex comedy" and thus serves as an approach to many comedies whose moral vision may be disagreeable to those he calls prudes, hypocrites, or stuffy academicians.

> The result in *The Country-Wife* is an immensely enjoyable play in which we take almost nothing seriously. Palmer exaggerates in saying that all questions of motive and moral value disappear: hypocrisy, affectation, and dissimulation enter too strongly to be ignored. Inspired buffoonery, though, is a fair description. Perhaps that phrase does less than justice to the ugliness and nasty quality often present in the play. But the critic may tend to forget just how much is plain farce. The gross character exaggerations are characteristic of farce, more than of comedy. Pinchwife is super-jealous, Sir Jaspar and Sparkish super-blind, Margery ultra-innocent, the ladies blatantly and exuberantly hypocritical. Margery dressed as her brother, Harcourt rigged out as a parson, the switched letters, the china scene, the substitution of Margery for Alithea, and the final resolution are all extraordinarily improbable and more the stuff of high farce than romantic comedy or serious satire. Delightfully bawdy and funny *The Country-Wife* is; profound it is not, and only a prude, a hypocrite, or a stuffy academician would have it otherwise. (P. 104)

Farce, Hume implies, is free from the traditional moral purposes of comedy. To call a comedy a farce is to exempt it from traditional critical scrutiny and interpretation, for in farce one does not seek theme or meaning or hope to locate metaphorical or symbolic levels of meaning. The *literal* dimension of its slapstick, buffoonery, double-entendres, and character types is its *only* dimension.

To classify *The London Cuckolds* as farce establishes one critical perspective, but it is not the only critical perspective one may use. Whether the plot is "perfectly immoral," as Nicoll says, may also depend on one's understanding of how cuckolding traditionally functioned in Medieval and Renaissance literature. To assume that Restoration literature is by definition different in kind from Medieval and Renaissance works is to measure cultural and artistic sensibility by a calendar, not by its social and aesthetic continuities. In "The Merchant's Tale," Chaucer in no way endorses adultery or even challenges traditional Christian assumptions about the value or importance of marital fidelity. As several critics have noted, Chaucer is less concerned with the varieties of lust than the power of pride to blind and to deceive.[11] January's lechery, his willful self-deception about his motives for marrying a young woman, his possessiveness of his youthful bride—all are factors that make his cuckolding "predictable and satisfactory. Our pleasure in this part of the story derives from seeing a generalized truth about human experience borne out— silly old men who marry lusty young wives will be cuckolded— and we silently congratulate ourselves that we live in a predictable universe where all remains as it should be."[12] Ravenscroft's moral universe is equally predictable.

Like Doodle, Wiseacre, and Dashwell, January is not merely cuckolded. His happiness is made dependent on his self-deception: a "glad" January, his vision not as beclouded as his understanding, leads May out of the garden. At the end of *The London Cuckolds* each husband is still "blind" to his relation to his wife, and despite the veracity of his friends' jibes, cannot accept that he has been cuckolded.

Dashwell. Now Mr. Alderman you see the effects of having a silly wife: And now I Hope at last you are convinced?
Wiseacre. No, no. ne're a whit, and so pray concern you your self with you [sic] zealous Wife there, who was above at her

	Devotions. And when the zealous fit was over, sent that Gentleman there to chastise you in the Garden for your folly....
Doodle.	... You may well scratch your Head, for all your Wives Vertue you'll see the fruits of her Zeal upon your fore-head ere long.
Dashwell.	I would not yet change my Wives Vertue for your Wives Wit, Mr. Alderman.
Doodle.	But Neighbour I think, *Consideratis Considerandis*, the Witty Wife is yet the best of the Three.
Dashwell.	To that I answer in your Wives own Dialect; *No*. (Pp. 59, 60)

Ravenscroft's emphasis on cuckolding, it could be argued, is no more prurient than Chaucer's tales of unhappy marriages. According to this critical perspective, cuckolding in comedy is a rhetorical means to a moral end, an aesthetic expression of a moral calculus: the humbling of vain, self-deceived men. More accurately, the moral vision of this comedy discloses the folly of men falsely proud of hoarding what is not theirs. The theme is thus paradoxical and witty: there are three ways for a fool to enshrine his wife's chastity, and none is successful. But if there be a "right way," to use Norman Holland's "right way-wrong way" axis, or if "virtue" or "honor" be possible in relations between men and women, then Ravenscroft does not show it.

In this reading of the comedy, the plot suggests a rather traditional moral vision. The reader sympathizes with wives (Eugenia and Peggy) forced to marry against their wills. Eugenia's servant Jane states the position in a homely way: "'Tis then your turn to please your self now with a Gallant, to supply the defects of a husband; when a man will press a woman to marry against her inclinations, he lays the foundation himself of being a Cuckold after" (p. 13). Where such enforced marriages are common—and it is clear that Eugenia's and Peggy's marriages were made against their will—and where the husbands are old, dull, and impotent, the husbands will be exceptionally jealous of their wives' fidelity, and the wives will be exceptionally interested in sexual adventure. The old men's blindness to the impropriety of January-May marriages and their hubris in believing that they can guarantee their wives' chastity create the comic situation, unite Ravenscroft's characters with those of Medieval *fabliaux* and Renaissance *novella,* and challenge the idea that Renaissance literature "ends" at the restoration of Charles II.

But Ravenscroft complicates the moral vision thus described when he translates traditional abstract ideas into dramatic characters. Clearly, the audience is to ridicule the aged lovers' vanity, pride, and blindness. But what response should be made to the three amorous couples who are created by the moral flaws of the old men? The couples, as I have argued above, are not idealized and do not represent or endorse any values except those associated with sensual pleasure.

Throughout the play, for example, Townly is as interested in wine as women. "Be rul'd by me," he counsels Ramble, "leave lewd whoring, and fall to honest drinking. . . . Wine don't disguise a man half so much as whoring, Ned" (pp. 34–35). Indeed, if Ramble wants to end his skein of unsuccessful intrigues, wine is the answer. "Wine gives a certain elevation of spirit, quickens and enlivens the fancy to that degree, that a man half bowsy shall advance farther with a woman in one encounter, than a sober fellow as thou art in ten, there's a certain boldness and alacrity wanting which lets a womans fancy sink and grow lukewarm when she was just boyling o'r" (p. 7) Ramble brags that he has been to church only for his father's funeral (p. 6) and to escape a rainstorm (p. 9); he seduces or, more likely, attempts to seduce three women in the play. His motive is not that he is a younger son and wishes to marry someone wealthy. He is not lonely, nor does he seek love. He merely wants a wench, and the wives of aldermen are eminently available. Loveday makes a slightly different claim on our attention: his parents had tricked him into forsaking Eugenia (p. 36), and Eugenia's loveless marriage could be made pitiable, but the odd mixture of youthful nostalgia, blackmail, and breathless passion in his seduction scene (pp. 36–37) reduces our sympathy for him. In less than sixty lines Loveday explains his machinations, revives her passion, acknowledges that her person is her husband's, and states that she cannot refuse his claim on her affection. He does not raise the problem of Eugenia's other suitors, who presumably lay equally valid claims on her affections. Such is the way of Ravenscroft's world.

With the exception of Peggy, a naïf more simpleminded and obtuse than pathetic, the young women are as similar as the young men. Eugenia and Arabella share the same disesteem for their husbands and differ only in the strategies by which they avoid arousing their husbands' suspicions. As Arabella says early in the play, referring to the need for discretion in managing her affairs, "This is not an age for the multiplication of fools in the female sex" (p. 5). Eugenia's ruse is piety: her effusive religious piety, her vigilant attendance at church, and her insatiable appetite for prayer successfully mask her real interests to her husband, if not to his friends. Arabella's wit is valued by her husband as his Maginot Line in the sexual warfare with the town's gallants. The two women's servants, Engine and Jane, merely echo their mistresses' values and thus require little separate discussion. Engine, for example, would like to marry only to cuckold her husband: "Oh the vain imaginations of a husband, who thinks himself secure of a wife, when he's in bed with her!—Oh were I but a wife, what ways wuld I invent to deceive a husband, and what pleasure I should take in this Roguery!" (p. 29). The women are unusually candid, even by Restoration standards, in disclosing their desires.

Arabella. Adieu, husband. A kiss! slender diet to live upon till to morrow this time: I have a months mind to greater dainties, to feast in his absence upon lustier fare than a dull City husband, as insipid and ill relisht as a *Guild hall*-dish on a Lord Mayor's day. . . .
Engine. A little variety, Madam, wou'd be pleasant; always to feed upon Alderman's flesh is enough to cloy your stomach.
Arabella. He's so sparking on't it can never surfeit me. (Pp. 5–6)

Lack of sexual activity and variety, Arabella confides, propels her into the arms of her many suitors. As Chaucer observed about another old husband's sexual prowess, the youthful wife "preyseth nat his pleyyng worth a bene."

But the comedy, however simple structurally, poses an interesting aesthetic and perceptual problem. At what point may the punishment of foolish old men be obscured by an endorsement of cuckolding as an end in itself? At what point may the reader's perception of the gallant as the instrument of deserved punishment change to a vision of the gallant as predator, as victim of his own moral defects or as both? The issue is crucial because what the reader "sees" in a text or in a performance determines the judgments that are reached. What we name something determines how we have judged or will judge it. In commenting on her work as loyal servant and perhaps as enterprising bawd, Engine implies that language determines our perception and thus the reality we see; by changing the language, we alter what is perceived, what in fact exists. She characterizes the "advanced" language of her own age and its concomitant way of understanding human experience.

> Let me see, what has my pains taking brought me in since morning 1—2—3—and 4—Guinies—When should I have got so much honestly on one day?—well this is a profitable profession, and in us that wait on Ladys the scandal is hid under the name of Cinfident or Woman: I would sooner choose to be some rich Lady's woman than many a poor Lord's Wife. This imployment was formerly stil'd Bawding and Pimping—but our Age is more civiliz'd—and our Language much refin'd—it is now a modish piece of service onely, and said, being compaisant, or doing a friend a kind of office. Whore—(oh filthy broad word!) is now prettily call'd Mistress;—Pimp, Friend; Cuckold-maker, Gallant: thus the terms being civiliz'd the thing becomes more practicable,—what Clowns they were in former Ages. (P. 27)

In the works of a Dryden, a Pope, or a Swift, such exuberant self-praise would be clearly ironic, and surely the lines lose much of their wit if not considered at least partly ironic, but I am uncertain whether they should be perceived as wholly so. They may also reflect the moral orientation of the play, an orientation that reflects the topsy-turvy ethical calculus of its fictive world. In reality, Engine says, whores are mistresses, gallants are cuckold-makers, and friends are pimps. Thus, despite the presence of plot formulas and character types traditionally used in Renaissance literature to "shadow forth" (in Sidney's words) an orthodox meaning, it is possible to perceive the three pairs of lovers as endorsements of the libertine's moral assumptions or, in modern terms, the sensibility of some modern philosophers and social scientists who "are convinced of the unparalleled significance of sex, both in individual psychology and in the evolution of civilization. . . . What makes them sexual radicals is their unqualified enthusiasm for sex, their belief that sexual pleasure is the ultimate measure of human happiness, and their pronounced hostility to the sexual repressiveness of modern civilization."[13] Ravenscroft's witty lovers, it seems to me, may sound a note that reverberates through three centuries of social psychology and ethical theory.

The London Cuckolds poses in clear terms problems obscured in more complex comedies of the period. The reader familiar with pre-Restoration literature recognizes in it components of traditional dramaturgy (the *senex amans*, the youthful and randy wife, the witty servant, the gallant), figures, and conventions of English and continental drama and narrative alike. But the reader also recognizes that there is no comic resolution or poetic justice that includes all who warrant punishment, say, as Jonson punishes characters' vices in *Volpone* or as Molière does in *Le Misanthrope*. Two of the husbands, Wiseacre and Dashwell, suffer physical pain, a traditional mode of punishment, but of the gallants only Ramble is made to look ridiculous: at various times he has a chamber pot emptied on his head; he is robbed, beaten, and blackened; he must fear for his "honor" (p. 32). The sins of these men, as Chaucer might say of his January or of the Miller and his cuckold, are of the flesh, and in the flesh they are punished. While just as culpable, Doodle and Townly escape physical punishment. A potentially orthodox moral vision thus conflicts with a traditional way of resolving this kind of plot. While each of the old fools is ridiculed and sometimes physically punished, the poetic justice that should be accorded the gallants is unevenly distributed, and the set of values represented by Eugenia and Arabella tends to overshadow the traditional meaning and pattern of justice that accompany a conventional cuckolding plot.

Thus, the task of analyzing the moral vision of this comedy is complicated by the conflict between the values enacted by the female characters and the plot, between the values that Arabella and Eugenia embody and the traditional plot of cuckolding a foolish husband. What distinguishes Arabella and Eugenia from Chaucer's May or Molière's Agnes is their extraordinary concupiscence: neither is interested in anything but sensual experience, flesh that does not cloy. Each is as promiscuous and devious as Ramble or Townly or Loveday, prowling the theatre, the street, or the church for suitable partners. Neither is disappointed when Ramble replaces Townly or Loveday substitutes for Ramble—or is it the other way around?—at an assignation. In creating Arabella and Eugenia, Ravenscroft molds traditional comic material—comic characters and plots—into a volatile new shape. The vitality and wit of Arabella and Eugenia finally overshadow the fact that Doodle-Wiseacre-Dashwell (these are but different names for the same character) deserves his fate, according to the conventions of a genre quite easily moralized in accord with orthodox seventeenth-century Christianity. What can function as a metaphor of pride in Chaucer cannot be easily seen as a metaphor in Ravenscroft. If its vision is to be regarded as moral by traditional standards, the comedy must be moralized, for at its literal level the characters who triumph compel no more approbation (except for their cleverness perhaps) than those who fail. But moralizing requires that much of the literal level of the comedy, especially the speech and action of Arabella and Eugenia, either be ignored or be interpreted as a metaphor that points to some orthodox scheme of values.

One such moralizing strategy is to perceive the comedy as a paradigm of what Richard King calls the party of Eros, a cluster of philosophical positions that regard the bedroom as the "battleground for change" (p. 8). By dramatizing the dynamics of sexual politics in such doggedly literal and graphic terms, by showing that the essence of sexual politics is the revolt of women against their economic and sexual enslavement, Ravenscroft foreshadows theorists like Goodman, Marcuse, and Brown in combining "a concern for instinctual and erotic liberation with political and social radicalism, cultural with political concern" (p. 50). Arabella's distaste is not just for her husband's flesh but for *alderman's* flesh, as "ill relisht as a *Guild hall*-dish on a Lord Mayor's day" (pp. 5–6). Just a few lines later Ramble describes Dashwell as a "Blockheaded-City Attorney; a Trudging, Drudging, Cormuging, Petitioning Citizen, that with a little Law and much Knavery has got a great Estate" (p. 8). And on numerous occasions the wits characterize themselves or are characterized as "Cavaliers," an identification with political reverberations not lost on Ravenscroft's first audience, which in November 1681 was agitated by the violence of Shaftesbury's faction of the city. For a cavalier to cuckold a Citizen, especially one both impotent and arrogant, was practically a political, if not a moral, imperative. That, according to this way of moralizing the comedy, would be a way to join erotic liberation and social radicalism, sweetening the bitter memories of the Civil War and Cromwellian austerity with the erotic fantasies and political concerns of the young people in this play.

But to appeal to such an abstraction takes us a very far distance from the play and requires us to ignore an important fact: aside from a few references, the women evince no political awareness and no sense of class consciousness. Their deep-breathing sex is indeed deep-breathing: no political or theological metaphors seem very probable constructs by which the play can be understood beyond its literal dimension. Only to the extent that the comedy can be read as a metaphor of the self-destructive nature of pride can *The London Cuckolds* be regarded as moral by traditional Christian standards. Plots, characters, and themes that Chaucer easily moralized lose their figurative and symbolic meaning, their potential for serving as allegories of the moral life, when translated into this idiom, vision, and genre. The alternative to moralizing this comedy is to moralize the *type* of play represented by *The London Cuckolds,* for to perceive such comedies as farce forestalls further aesthetic and moral considerations. And even if *The London Cuckolds* can legitimately be considered a farce, such plays as *The Country Wife* raise similar aesthetic questions.

Unlike *The London Cuckolds*, Wycherley's *The Country Wife* has received a great amount of critical attention, most of it favorable, from modern critics. The plots of both plays fuse the gulling and fornication plots common in earlier comedy; both plays feature the vain attempts of mean, jealous husbands to avoid cuckoldom and the intrigues of their wives who seek horns for their husbands; both plays present gallants whose ingenuity is challenged by the women they court, a naïf who has been especially "schooled" by her elderly husband, and a witwoud who is cozened by another gallant. But *The Country Wife* is more complex structurally and thematically: it offers a romantic subplot that is complicated not by the usual blocking figure, a husband or an overzealous father or brother, but by Alithea's own sense of abstract moral obligation to Sparkish, who is clearly unsuited to her. Horner, a more complicated gallant than Townly, Ramble, or Loveday, is contrasted in style and motive with Harcourt and Sparkish, who are also engaged in courtship. Because of their obvious similarities and striking differences, it is useful to consider these comedies in juxtaposition.

A major disagreement among critics of *The Country Wife* is their perception of Horner's nature and dramatic significance. To understand Horner implies an apprehension of the characters with whom he competes and contrasts, the nature of the actions he initiates, and the outcome, triumphant or pyrrhic, of his ruse. Two recent analyses of Horner by modern critics suggest the diversity of perception even among those who admire the play.

> Horner is (and in part by virtue of his very "wickedness") a wholly positive and creative comic hero, and . . . much of the imagery of the play places him squarely on the side of health, of freedom, and most controversial of all, of honesty. (Birdsall, *Wild Civility*, p. 136)

> Horner is undeniably a bad man who does bad things, but he is not a villain in the sense that, say, Iago, is, for he does not prey on innocents. The people Horner victimizes, his cuckolds and mistresses, are

Critical Practice

either far worse than he, or, like Margery, do not feel that they have been harmed. (Holland, *The First Modern Comedies*, p. 75)

Birdsall and Holland initially agree that Horner is "wicked," apparently a clear moral judgment that may imply a basis for judging other characters (i.e., to argue that Horner is less reprehensible than Pinchwife implies a moral continuum and gradations of evil), but Birdsall regards his wickedness as a sign of creativity and vitality, elements that align Horner with health, freedom, and the other *honnêtes hommes* of his century. To Holland, the Fidgets' lust and Margery's willingness to be seduced reduce Horner's culpability. The conflict between those critics emphasizes a fundamental division among ways of seeing the play: is it exemplary comedy (Birdsall), satiric comedy (Holland, Fujimura, and Zimbardo), or farce (Palmer and Hume)? Just as important is a second question less frequently considered: on what basis and with what kind of evidence does a critic classify *The Country Wife* as satiric, exemplary, or farcical?

In seventeenth-century accounts of comedy, as Singh and others have noted, the theory and purpose of comedy are relatively simple.[14] Comedy is didactic, teaching or reforming by exposing to ridicule the foibles of the foolish and the vices of the wicked. The audience, it is presumed, discerns the foible or vice that is attacked or the virtue that is recommended and is led thereby to eschew what is improper and to emulate the values the dramatist endorses. What happens, however, if the debauched characters seem attractive to the audience, if the satiric punishment is so gentle or ambiguous or incomplete that it is not perceived by the audience? It would seem that in this case the play would endorse the debauched character and the values he represents, or the play would be considered a failure because it inadequately represents the vision the author wanted to convey. Or it could mean that the lineaments of poetic justice required by some critics (Collier) are so blatantly obvious and heavy-handed that they are dramatically unworkable. One of Jeremy Collier's strongest charges against Restoration comedy was that it rewarded the vicious characters and ridiculed the virtuous. Birdsall and Holland, defenders of the moral vision of these plays, have responded to this charge in quite different ways, and the importance of this question can be suggested by noting that the debate surfaces whenever a morally ambiguous position is apparently endorsed in a work (as in the movie *Dirty Harry*) or when quite contradictory moral positions seem to be equally well supported by a work (the movies of Sam Peckinpah).

A modern example of this problem will perhaps clarify the aesthetic problem that Horner poses. In the critical furor that surrounded the first episodes of *All in the Family* a few years ago, the character of Archie Bunker seemed almost as protean as Harry Horner's, and the supposed *effects* of Archie's popularity stimulated both dire predictions and guarded optimism among the critics of the series and social commentators at large. Archie, like Horner, discloses his values and intentions forthrightly and unapologetically to the audience, and one can assume that at least some of the audience share them. Archie feels that he knows the world, its pretenses, and its underlying reality. In a society whose moral values are unsettled because of rapid social change, Archie is defiantly proud to be a male chauvinist, a blue-collar worker, and a moonlighting bootstrapper who resents the apparent advantages of blacks, Jews, Catholics, liberals, Communists, non-Americans, and non-fundamentalists. An early review of the series suggested that the show "may either polarize the country beyond measure or successfully treat the issue of bigotry in terms of laughter,"[15] thereby ascribing nearly the same power to instruct and reform that seventeenth-century theorists attributed to their comic literature.

Accepting the premise that a half-hour comedy could wield enormous social power, the late Whitney Young, Jr. of the Urban League saw the popularity of the series as an endorsement of Archie Bunker's values and felt that Archie's presence in millions of American homes popularized the bigotry that the series ostensibly attacked. "It is reprehensible," he said, "to air a show like this at a time when our nation is polarized and torn by racism."[16] The problem with *All in the Family* (or *The Country Wife*) is that satire does not necessarily inhere in a text: it must be perceived in order to exist. Many in the audience may see only humor in Archie's emotional excesses and the implausible or ludicrous situations that he creates for himself. Others may see Archie as a hero, a defender of cherished values seemingly discredited by many in our society. Still others may see the show as satiric and Archie as the butt of the satire because the comic situations of which he is the victim are nearly always the result of his own moral and social values. When he objects to the sexual permissiveness of the young (while he endorses a double standard for older males) or the vanity of women (while he preens himself before a mirror), Archie may be seen either as a sympathetic victim or a vicious bigot, and what we call him depends on how we see him. What we see in him depends partly on what we choose to see and partly on what the comedy insists that we observe.

Norman Lear, the creator of the series, has capitalized on the ambiguity of this perceptual dilemma by making Archie, as he says, a "lovable bigot" like his own father.[17] Thus, Archie's bigotry is softened if we are made to sympathize with him; his racism, sexism, and other vices are made more understandable and perhaps less objectionable if the audience regards Archie sympathetically rather than critically. If Archie is seen as lovable, then it is difficult for him to serve as a satiric butt, an embodiment of parochial, benighted, or vicious values. Since Archie Bunker is a complexly realized character, not an abstract embodiment of virtue or vice, his familiarity and vitality make it uncertain that his loyal audience will discern and repudiate the bigoted values he represents. As in Restoration comedy, admiration of or sympathy for a central character blurs the satiric focus and brings into serious question the rhetorical effect and moral vision of the work.

If *The Country Wife* is regarded as a satire, one must necessarily locate an object or objects of satire. One could argue plausibly that such vices or foibles as lust, jealousy, pretension, hypocrisy, or exploitative marital conventions might be the focus of Wycherley's *saeva indignatio,* but it is difficult to be comfortable with such an approach. Clearly, the vices are present in the comedy, but none seems preeminent. Moreover, Horner seems to escape the satirist's lash even though he seems as vicious as the characters whom he "exposes." As Hume notes in a brilliant insight, in *The Development of English Drama in the Late Seventeenth Century*, if Wycherley had wanted to satirize lust, it would have been simple to conclude the play by having Horner get the pox and become impotent, wrapping the comedy in a rich level of irony: at last the trickster is tricked, the lustful one burned by the passion by which he inflamed others (p. 99). But *The Country Wife* does not end this way, and the problem of how to perceive the comedy is not solved by arbitrarily assigning a particular vice or set of vices as the central theme or problem of the play.

In an essay published several years ago, Hume provides a helpful framework for identifying the aesthetic problem presented by the play. He proposes that comedies can be differentiated by noting the kinds of responses they are designed to produce.[18] The amount of admiration of and affection for the characters determines our response to the play. Is Horner a lovable rake or a dissolute lecher? On one extreme of this continuum are characters whom the audience is to admire and emulate (as in Steele's *The Conscious Lovers*); on the other extreme are characters who are ridiculed and to whom the audience feels superior, enjoying "the antics of fools and knaves, but [holding] them in contempt" (p. 92). Characters in such plays as Aristophanes' *The Clouds* or *Volpone* would illustrate this range of response. Between the extremes are two groups: characters for whom the audience feels "nominal sympathy" (as in *The Beaux Strategem*) but with whose interests it does not identify; and characters whom "we like, enjoy and identify with . . . in a serious way" (p. 92), as in *Much Ado About Nothing*. Obviously, these categories are not absolute, but they do allow the critic to locate his response to Wycherley's characters, especially to Horner and Harcourt, somewhere on a continuum from contempt to affection. In essence, the response is based not only upon a moral judgment of and psychological identification with the characters, but also on a judgment of the moral coherence of the fictional world that includes these characters.

Critical Practice

What can be said of Harry Horner and the world in which he lives? Horner exploits the moral paradoxes at the center of the plot: if a man wants to enjoy complete sexual freedom, he should advertise his impotence by swearing his physician to secret-mongering; if a husband wants to insure that his wife is faithful, he should seek a country wife or provide a eunuch for his city wife; if a woman wants to enjoy sexual freedom, she should proclaim her prudery and blush at the mention of "naked." The play opens swiftly with Horner's disclosure of his ruse to an incredulous doctor. Indeed, one of the aspects of this play that has gone unnoted is the function of the doctor in testing the values by which Horner lives and identifying the values by which Horner judges others and by which he may himself be judged.

In the opening scene the doctor expresses his reservations about Horner's plans. "You take, methinks, a very preposterous way to it, and as ridiculous as if we operators in physic should put forth bills to disparage our medicaments, with hopes to gain customers."[19] No virtuoso in physic or metaphysics, the doctor reasonably expects that appearance approximates reality and that social relations obey laws as immutable and inviolable as those of his laboratory. After seeing Horner's mysogyny and effrontery to Lady Fidget, he is even more dubious.

Quack. Now, I think, I, or you yourself rather, have done your business with the women.
Horner. Thou art an ass. Don't you see already, upon the report and my carriage, this grave man of business leaves his wife in my lodgings, invites me to his house and wife, who before would not be acquainted with me out of jealousy?
Quack. Nay, by this means you may be the more acquainted with the husbands, but the less with the wives.
Horner. Let me alone; if I can but abuse the husbands, I'll soon disabuse the wives....
Quack. Nay, now you shall be the doctor; and your process is so new that we do not know but it may succeed.
Horner. Not so new neither; probatum est, doctor.
Quack. Well, I wish you luck and many patients whilst I go to mine.
(Pp. 10–11)

What *The Country Wife* provides for the doctor and the audience, which may be as skeptical as the doctor about Horner's experiment, is a test of a new procedure, a new chemistry, for procuring mistresses. Horner has become the doctor, the chemist of human relations, and his alembic is the social world reflected in Sir Jasper and his women, Pinchwife, and Sparkish. The doctor's reservations are sensible and prudent, well grounded in commonsense expectations about the relations of men and women. The "education" of the doctor in the ways of the world may mime the kind of education that the comedy offers to its audience.

The audience can chart the doctor's progress and perhaps glimpse its own by considering the doctor's other two appearances in the comedy, both at critical moments in Horner's experiment. In Act IV the doctor asks Horner, "how fadges the new design? Have you not the luck of all your brother projectors, to deceive only yourself at last?" (p. 92). Horner swears that his ploy has made him privy to the secret lives of honorable wives, whom the doctor assumes do not sing bawdy songs or drink excessively. This is not the case, says Horner, as he invites the doctor to observe him in his laboratory. "For your bigots in honor are just like those in religion; they fear the eye of the world more than the eye of Heaven, and think there is no virtue but railing at vice, and no sin but giving scandal. They rail at a poor, little, kept player, and keep themselves some young, modest pulpit comedian to be privy to their sins in their closets, not to tell 'em of them in their chapels" (pp. 92–93).

More important than his *claims* about the world is Horner's *probatum est,* his empirical demonstration, to the curious physician. As the doctor slips behind the screen, Lady Fidget enters and begins the famous "china scene," after which the doctor confides in an aside to the audience, "I will now believe anything he tells me" (p. 101). The significance of this aside should be stressed, for if the doctor initially represents the skeptical sensibility of the audience, which presumably does not harbor such dour sentiments about the beau monde as Horner proclaims, then his "education" attests to Horner's credibility as a chemist

Critical Practice

who has accurately analyzed the society in which he lives. The lab report that Horner presents in all of its luridly clinical detail also delineates Horner's criteria for moral judgment. And if the doctor has any lingering doubts about Horner's analysis, they are dispelled when he observes the horning of Pinchwife, the most jealous husband in the play. That scene corroborates Horner's assumptions about the nature of his world, so henceforth the doctor will think it "not impossible for [Horner] to cuckold the Grand Signior admit his guards of eunuchs" (p. 106). In short, the doctor's prior knowledge of human chemistry was inadequate, and in light of Horner's experiment, he must abandon his discredited assumptions.

In the doctor's appearance in the closing scene, the doctor is drawn from mere observation of to active participation in Horner's scheme. The cuckolds are about to expose the fraud, threatening both their own illusions about themselves and their wives' pretensions, so the doctor must protect Horner's fantasy. He does this by duplicating Horner's laboratory technique, which relies on the synergy of hearsay, illusion, and social pressure to conjure reality: "Gentlemen and ladies, han't you all heard the late sad report of poor Mr. Horner?" (p. 139). All of the women except Margery respond predictably to this cue.

Lady Fidget.	Upon my honor, sir, 'tis as true—
Mrs. Dainty Fidget.	D'ye think we would have been seen in his company?
Mrs. Squeamish.	Trust our unspotted reputations with him! (P. 139)

And in the next line Horner remarks proudly in an aside to the doctor, "Well, doctor, is not this a good design, that carries a man on unsuspected, and brings him off safe?" (p. 139). This line is the *probatum est* of the experiment Horner proposed to the doctor in the opening scene. The hypothesis has been tested and the results have been confirmed and replicated before the doctor's eyes: given Horner's nature and the nature of his world, a character like Horner can manipulate reality so adroitly that he can gain whatever he wants. Newton's laws were to be no less precise in predicting and explaining the operations of physical nature.

What, though, has been proven? The play confirms Horner's hypothesis that in a world in which honor is but a word and virtue but a pose, whoever dissimulates most successfully will acquire most power and will least likely be a victim of others' ruthless schemes. The play would seem to corroborate Horner's assumptions about human nature except that Harcourt also achieves his goal—marriage to Alithea—without stooping to Horner's level. Indeed, to contrast Harcourt's values with Horner's is to see that within *The Country Wife* are two quite separate worlds, responsive to quite different sets of expectations about the basis of marriage and the importance of love. What Horner "proves" is true of his world, but his world is not large enough to include Harcourt and Alithea, whose unique relationship requires separate consideration. Horner's world is not the world of sex, although Hume classifies *The Country Wife* as a "sex comedy," but of gaming. Sex is sought, offered, or withheld not for its own sake but as a means of enhancing one's power over others through calculated risks.

In fact, the language of gaming even serves as an analogy of sexual experience: a marriage vow, says Horner,

>is like a penitent gamester's oath, and entering into bonds and penalties to stint himself to such a particular small sum at play for the future, which makes him but the more eager, and not being able to hold out, loses his money again, and his forfeit to boot.
>
>*Dorilant.* Ay, ay, a gamester will be a gamester whilst his money lasts, and a whore master whilst his vigor.
>*Harcourt.* Nay, I have known 'em, when they are broke and can lose no more, keep a-fumbling with the box in their hands to fool with only, and hinder other gamesters.
>*Dorilant.* That had wherewithal to make lusty stakes. (P. 22)

Pinchwife wants to marry a country wife as insurance against being cuckolded. He marries, in fact, only because he could never keep a whore to himself (p. 23), and a country wife is a better choice than a witty wife: "'Tis my maxim, he's a fool that marries, but he's a greater that does not marry a fool. What is wit in a wife good for, but to make a man a cuckold?" (p. 21). Put another way, Pinchwife risks marriage only to control another's sexual activity, and this control, real or imaginary, defines his interest in Margery and characterizes his gamble. Sir Jasper confesses that his pleasure is business while the business of women is pleasure (p. 47). Four lines after this statement his wife stresses *her* understanding of the business/pleasure dichotomy: "Who for his business from his will run,/Takes the best care to have her business done" (p. 48). Lady Fidget sees her gamble with Horner as retribution for her husband's neglect (p. 38) and her reputation for virtue as like "the statesman's religion, the Quaker's word, the gamester's oath, and the great man's honor—but to cheat those that trust us" (p. 128). To ensure her fidelity and to provide the companionship he withholds, Sir Jasper gleefully adopts Horner as his sterile supernumerary, the eunuch in his seraglio. Again the language of business permeates his thinking. "Business must be preferred always before love and ceremony with the wise, Mr. Horner. . . . 'Tis as much a husband's prudence to provide innocent diversion for a wife as to hinder her unlawful pleasure, and he had better employ her than let her employ herself" (pp. 9–10).

In the battle between Horner, the women, and their husbands, sex is not the focus but the medium of exchange, a commodity that is preserved or traded for tactical reasons and is itself a symbol of power and control. For example, because the reputation for virtue is important for the freedom it confers, the reported loss of virtue is catastrophic. Men of honor know this, Mrs. Dainty Fidget tells Horner, and

> do satisfy their vanity upon us sometimes; and are unkind to us in their report, tell all the world they lie with us.
>
> *Lady Fidget.* Damned rascals! That we should be wronged by 'em; to report a man has had a person, when he has not had a person, is the greatest wrong in the whole world that can be done to a person. (P. 39)

Sexual slander is especially deplorable to the women because it preempts their use of virtue, real or reported, in furthering private designs. The fact of sexual virtue, Horner tells Pinchwife, is less significant than the reputation of virtue because if a wife "cannot make her husband a cuckold, she'll make him jealous, and pass for one, and then 'tis all one" (p. 22).

If Horner successfully reveals the foolishness of Sir Jasper, Sparkish, Pinchwife, and Lady Fidget and her entourage, how then does the audience regard him? Does the response lean more toward affection and esteem (after all, Horner has exposed the cant of the hypocrites and tortured a mean, jealous husband), contempt for his own dishonorable behavior, or indifference? As the catalyst for the two cuckolding plots, he compels attention, and the audience, like the doctor, is drawn into his intrigues by the boldness of his designs and their high probability of failure. Whether Horner is laboring in his china shop within earshot of Sir Jasper or mediating the potential rivalry of the *grandes dames,* the illusions on which his ruse depends are always near collapse. If Sir Jasper *believes* his eyes (as January did not) or if Margery is allowed to describe explicitly her evidence of Horner's potency, then his world explodes and with it the gossamer web of respectability in which the other major characters (except for Harcourt and Alithea) are wrapped.

As the generator of comic action and dramatic tension, Horner compels attention and perhaps a certain admiration for the wit and cunning intelligence by which he avoids detection and punishment. But Horner is never a likable character, much less a lovable one. The audience can see, for example, that his values are no less acquisitive or manipulative or selfish than those of his victims. Indeed, his success depends on the same affectation, hypocrisy, and lust that he unmasks in others. His wit, resourcefulness, and energy make him fascinating to watch, but his vices are repellent, unmitigated, and fully disclosed to the audience from the opening scene. His ratiocination for lying about his involvement with Alithea, which he makes in an aside to the audience that sits in judgment of Wycherley's world, is simple and direct: "Now must I wrong one woman for another's sake, but that's no new thing with me; for in these cases I am still on the criminal's side, against the innocent" (p. 133). He confesses to Lady Fidget that he is a "Machiavel in love" (p. 94), meaning that like Machiavelli's prince, he seeks power over others as an end in itself. He recognizes no obligations to anyone else and will use any ruse, however outrageous or treacherous, to gain whatever or whomever he covets. And when Horner speaks of women and love, his imagery is characteristically base: "ceremony in love and eating is as ridiculous as in fighting; falling on briskly is all should be done in those occasions" (p. 127). In summary, the virtues of wit and energy are as clear in Horner as the vices of lust, vanity, and hypocrisy. While Horner's ruse may serve as a mirror in which other characters may glimpse their own deformities, it is also a glass that magnifies the vices within.

Given such a mixture of characters, Wycherley's vision may not be discerned easily since the critic still must decide whether the comedy is satiric, exemplary, or farcical. Hume, who is clearly aware of the implications of genre in understanding Restoration comedy, sees the play as heavily satiric yet without "a systematic ethical didacticism" (*Development,* p. 99) from which the satire derives its moral norms. His approach is to see the play as satiric in tone but a farce by genre, an argument advanced in quite different language early in this century by John Palmer. "*The Country-Wife* is an immensely enjoyable play in which we take almost nothing seriously. Palmer exaggerates in saying that all questions of motive and moral value disappear: hypocrisy, affectation, and dissimulation enter too strongly to be ignored. Inspired buffoonery, though, is a fair description. Perhaps that phrase does less than justice to the ugliness and nasty quality often present in the play. But the critic may tend to forget just how much is plain farce" (*Development,* p. 104).

Hume's approach moralizes the comedy not by denying Horner's wickedness or by seeing him as on the side of health and freedom (Birdsall) or by stressing the satiric elements (Fujimura, Holland, and Zimbardo) but by denying it seriousness (Palmer and Lamb). Unlike Palmer and Lamb, Hume does not postulate an aesthetics of cloud-cuckoo land for his interpretation. Although recognizing the satiric elements, he finally does not classify it as a satire. But by seeing the comedy as farce, he forestalls other considerations, since farce is not generally regarded as having a moral vision of any critical interest. By grouping *The Country Wife* with other farces, Hume restricts his focus to what he is likely to see, even though a prude, hypocrite, or stuffy academician, to use his terms, might just as likely see other elements if he had expected to find a satiric or an exemplary comedy rather than a farce.

The argument that a comedy dealing unconventionally with sexual themes is a farce imposes an enormous burden on a critic who does not see the work as a farce but as a "serious" enactment of moral values. How does one measure the degree of seriousness? How much seriousness is sufficient to make the work a comedy and not a farce? I have demonstrated that despite surface similarities, *The Country Wife* and *The London Cuckolds* are quite different plays thematically and structurally. But to argue that *The Country Wife* is a farce with satiric elements added is to understate what Wycherley seemed intent on establishing: the pattern of justice to which each character is entitled. For their jealousy and obtuseness, Pinchwife and Sir Jasper are tortured with horns, real or imaginary ("'tis all one"); for lack of wit and purblind vanity, Sparkish is deprived of his betrothed and roundly ridiculed by the more successful suitor; the great ladies have been exposed to each other for what they are; Alithea and Harcourt, having suffered the pains of all idealized lovers, find love and marriage possible within the same relationship; and Horner remains himself, an ambulatory dildo at least as much manipulated by the women as he is a manipulator of them. As the play closes, every important male character except Sir Jasper responds tellingly to Lucy's observation, "any wild thing grows but the more fierce and hungry for being kept up, and more dangerous to the keeper" (p. 139). The responses differentiate the "reward" each has received.

Alithea. There's doctrine for all husbands, Mr. Harcourt.
Harcourt. I edify, madam, so much that I am impatient till I am one.
Dorilant. And I edify so much by example I will never be one.
Sparkish. And because I will not disparage my parts I'll ne'er be one.
Horner. And I, alas, can't be one.

Pinchwife. But I must be one—against my will, to a country wife, with a country murrain to me. (P. 140).

Horner, I stress, declares that he cannot be a husband. Does Horner mean that in comparison with Harcourt's love for Alithea, he will never be able to love or to marry? Does he mean that his grim insights into married life make him unable ever to contemplate marriage? Does he mean that he expects to continue his role à la capon and thus can never consider marriage? The interpretation partly depends on the actor's presentation of the line, for even "alas" can be either ironic or sincere. If Horner pauses and turns serious for a moment, then he suggests an awareness of his own mechanical sterility; if he is flippant, then his merriment at the end of the play is genuine and he is not merely covering his trail with the diverting spectacle of dance.

It is significant that Wycherley ends the comedy in a dance of cuckolds. Instead of concluding with a wedding dance, appropriate to a play whose subplot is romantic and thus symbolizes the order and social stability that marriage is thought to support, Wycherley offers a dance of cuckolds, an icon of disorder, of loyalties forsaken and vows neglected. When the maskers dance, they affirm only their own individuality. Nothing binds one to another, even though the idea of a dance requires some type of order or some system of pattern and movement to which all participants have agreed. It is possible to see the conclusion as Wycherley's version of the Don Juan theme: rather than being dragged off to Hell, Horner finds Hell where he is, confinement to his own solitary being and the petty illusions by which he defines himself and of which he is master.[20]

But does Horner receive his due? The ambiguity of his situation at the end of the play has invited the extraordinary range of critical opinion on the meaning of this comedy. If the critic can accurately assume that the audience will be more disgusted by Horner than attracted to him, then the moral direction is clear and is underscored by the successful union of Harcourt and Alithea. The inclusion of an idealized romantic couple is significant as a rejection of Horner's values. Harcourt contrasts sharply with Horner, Sparkish, and Pinchwife in his intentions and tactics. While Sparkish is "tricked" by Harcourt, he is the only character unable to see Harcourt's affection for Alithea and his marital ambitions. Moreover, Harcourt's intentions are marriage, not seduction, throughout the comedy. His beloved Alithea blocks his suit not because she rejects his love but because she embraces an abstract, narrowly defined conception of her obligations to Sparkish. Only the timely intervention of Lucy enables her to see the perils of marriage to Sparkish and to escape from him before vows are taken. In Wycherley's world, while happy marriage is not typical, it is at least possible, something that cannot be said of Ravenscroft's world, and it is made to seem desirable. But marriage of this kind is clearly not possible for Horner, Sir Jasper, Pinchwife, or the *grandes dames*.

The critical disagreement over Horner's nature and thus the kind of response the play elicits indicates that the moral vision is by no means clear or, for many in the audience, predictable. Furthermore, no interpretation of this comedy is likely to be persuasive unless critics can agree whether they are seeing a satiric comedy, an exemplary comedy, or a farce. It is quite possible that *The Country Wife*, like *The London Cuckolds* or *Deep Throat* or *All in the Family*, can be moralized and made to fit almost any critical scheme. But no critic is likely to convince another that his interpretation is superior until critics understand more clearly why they "see" works of imaginative literature as they do and consider the variety of ways in which literature can be regarded as moral.[21]

If one sees *The Country Wife* or *The London Cuckolds* only on a literal level, then the "moral facts" should be easily identified and the moral evaluation that ensues should be predictable. Moral judgments, after all, are tautological: when one has discovered the moral facts of a case, then the judgment emerges automatically from the perception of the facts. The critic's approval of the moral vision of a work rests on the compatibility of his values with those he sees expressed in the work. But if imaginative literature is seen as symbolic, as an artifact capable of multiple dimensions of meaning, then the task of ascertaining the moral facts is much more formidable. For one thing, the critic must realize that the metaphoric meaning he perceives is partly a function of the text, partly a function of his own sensibility, and partly a function of his own expectations about the work.

When literature is seen within the context of genres and understood within the traditions by which different genres embody their vision and meaning, the critic encounters the problem of defending his perception and interpretation of the metaphor that he sees expressed by the work. In the Reformation debate over the meaning of the Song of Solomon, for example, commentators disagreed about the literal versus symbolic nature of its language as sharply as modern exegetes of Restoration comedy have clashed over its moral vision. Was the Song of Solomon metaphoric, thus symbolizing the love of God and man or Christ and the Church? Or was it starkly literal, an erotic colloquy between Solomon and his beloved Shulamite? The commentators were aware that orthodox meaning, the moral vision of the text, hinged on the perception of metaphor. In moralizing this troublesome text, one Reformation commentator proclaimed: "away . . . with all carnal thoughts, while we have heavenly things presented us under the notion of Kisses, Lips, Breasts, Navel, Belly, Thighs, Leggs. Our minds must be above our selves, altogether minding heavenly meanings."[22]

In the commentary on Song of Solomon 5:4 ("My beloved put in his hand by the hole *of the door,* and my bowels were moved for him"), another commentator nervously noted that "to an impure fancy this verse is more apt to foment lewd and base lusts, than to present holy and divine notions. . . . It is shameful to mention what foul ugly rottenness some have belched here and how they have neglected that pure and Christian sense that is clear in the words." The gulf between Calvin and Sebastian Castellio over this matter is no greater than the gulf between those critics who see *The Country Wife* as farcical and those who see it as exemplary or as satirical.

At a symbolic level, *The Country Wife* and *The London Cuckolds* are more than exposés, however witty, of manners and values.

But the moral facts about these works are less easily articulated because both plays may bear symbolic levels of meaning, thus undercutting the significance of their literal meaning. If the cuckolding that occupies the surface structures of the plays is seen as a metaphor of pride, then the plays are easily moralized: Horner's role in the play and the concept of "honor" that he reflects define the curriculum in his school for husbands, a curriculum of moral assumptions about decorum and human nature that existed long before the restoration of Charles II. Thus, Horner is less a character than a rhetorical *donnée* of the genre. His efforts at deep-breathing sex are inspired and sustained by derelict husbands, who, according to the conventions of the genre, must cuckold themselves at least once so that they may know the sting of pride. The comedy is "immoral and profane" only when perceived as a literal endorsement of Horner's Machiavellian ethos and when the significance of Harcourt's successful courtship is disregarded. To see Horner as a victim of his own sterility, of his own literary conventionality, places him and the comedy in quite another critical perspective.

6

"Duels, Claps, and Bastards": The Problem of Sympathy and Judgment

> The fundamental act of criticism is a disinterested response to a work of literature in which all one's beliefs, engagements, commitments, prejudices, stampedings of pity and terror, are ordered to be quiet. We are now dealing with the imaginative, not the existential, with "let this be," not with "this is," and no work of literature is better by virtue of what it says than any other work. Such a disinterested response takes rigorous discipline, and many, even among skilled critics, never consistently attain it. But the fact that it is there to be attained can hardly be disputed. (Northrop Frye, *The Well-Tempered Critic*)

> A writer writes a novel, a poet writes a poem, to find out what he can honestly maintain, not just with his head but with all his nature. He gives it to readers not only to delight them and instruct them but also to support them if they are the right kind of people already and stir doubts if they're not.... Art is our way of keeping track of what we know and have known, secretly, from the beginning. It is precisely because art affirms values that it is important. (John Gardner, *On Moral Fiction*)

If *The Country Wife* and *The London Cuckolds* exploit the conventions of what Robert D. Hume calls "sex comedy,"[1] then they necessarily invite a broad range of critical discussion because such comedies raise questions of values and beliefs important to critics and society alike. Whether critics are capable of the "disinterested response" that Frye idealizes is a serious aesthetic question, but whether a "disinterested criticism" would prove valuable and interesting cannot be answered until this sublime disengagement is achieved. Nor does such a position help the critic interested in the moral vision of particular comedies, especially those whose themes or conventions are puzzling or seem distasteful. Turning away from plays whose major action involves cuckolding to comedies concerned with other ethical problems, we see the centrality of the authors' concern for raising and answering moral questions. Thomas Otway's *The Souldiers Fortune* (1680) and *The Atheist* (1682) and Thomas Shadwell's *The Squire of Alsatia* (1688) were successful with their contemporary audiences but have been largely ignored by most modern critics, who define the "canon" of Restoration comedy as the works of five other authors. Regardless of their striking differences Otway and Shadwell offer comic visions both complex and incisive. Though both comedies end with the prospect of marriage, neither author implies an easy accommodation to conventional affirmations of marriage or the likelihood of human happiness.

No Restoration comedy should be "read" as a moral tract or a philosophical treatise. Every comedy would fail if compared to the rhetorical effectiveness of Hobbes or Temple or Savile. But comic drama does enact ideas and encourage attitudes *toward* ideas through patterns of dramatic action, resolution (or nonresolution) of conflicts among characters, and distribution of rewards and punishment. Comic visions can be discerned as we recognize the ways in which authors introduce and define ethical problems and then resolve—or leave unresolved—the problems confronted by the major characters. From this perspective, then, let me focus first on ethical concerns in Otway and Shadwell, concerns that become particularly evident in Otway's treatment of justice and friendship and Shadwell's view of raising children who have the proper sense of moral responsibility. Then I place in a broader perspective the critical questions that have shaped my discussion of these plays and my earlier discussion of *The*

The Problem of Sympathy and Judgment

Country Wife and *The London Cuckolds*. While the most basic claims about the "moral" effects of literature—claims central to the *moralisé* tradition of criticism—remain unsubstantiated, I conclude by suggesting some lines of inquiry that may prove useful in clarifying the relation of imaginative literature to its audience.

Of Thomas Otway's comedies, Dr. Johnson has almost nothing to say, dismissing them in only one sentence while telling at length several unhappy versions of Otway's final days. Although modern critics have been more interested in the tragedies than the comedies, Hume properly emphasizes the importance of Otway's bitterly satiric tone in his comedies.[2] Unlike such plays as *The London Cuckolds* or Durfey's *A Fond Husband*, *The Souldiers Fortune* uses the conventions of the cuckolding plot, by this time very familiar to London audiences, as part of a larger rhetorical design. What makes Otway's comedy sharply different from other "sex comedies" popular in the 1680s is the careful development of an aesthetics of voyeurism. Wycherley had titillated audiences with Horner's "china" scene, and the sight of more than one person hiding in a closet or under a bed during a seduction scene was not unusual. Otway's innovation was Sir Jolly Jumble, whose boundless energy and prurient frenzy direct the course of the cuckolding plot, entice the audience to participate in his sexual fantasies, and undercut the optimism generated by the Courtine-Sylvia romance.

On the surface, *The Souldiers Fortune* seems rather like other comedies of the 1670s and 1680s. A young woman, Clarinda, is forced to marry Sir Davy Dunce, who is rich, impotent, and aged, thereby forsaking Beaugard, who is poor, virile, and young. Such a marriage invites the *senex amans* to be cuckolded, and the witty lovers provide him the opportunity. Since the "justice" of the cuckolding plot is a *donnée* of this genre, Otway concentrates on embellishing a plot structure and altering a comic vision already very familiar to his audience. A subplot, Courtine's courtship of Sylvia, is one part of the embellishment, for their marriage initially suggests that the play is attacking bad marriages, not marriage itself. Good marriages are possible and are the "solution" to the problems created by bad marriages.[3]

But with the introduction of Sir Jolly Jumble, Otway's comedy grows significantly more complex and its vision darkens.

Sir Jolly Jumble, played brilliantly by Mr. Leigh in the first production at the Duke's Theatre in 1680, is surely one of the oddest characters on the Restoration stage. Shadwell's Snarl, whose masochism is displayed in *The Virtuoso,* and Lee's Nemours, whose vices are depicted in *The Princess of Cleve,* are clearly presented as repellent characters and viciously satirized. But Sir Jolly Jumble is not only unpunished for his vices; he prospers because of them. From his first moments on the stage, Sir Jolly seems to be a creature from a universe quite different from the world so unfair to Courtine, Fourbin, and Beaugard (soldiers who had served their country and who then found themselves penniless and scorned). As domineering and conniving as he is perverse, Sir Jolly's priapic energy leads the audience to see him, in Courbin's words, as the "most extraordinary rogue" they have ever seen.

Sir Jolly. My Hero! my darling! my *Ganimede!* how dost thou? Strong! wanton! lusty! rampant! hah, ah, ah! She's thine Boy, odd she's thine, plump, soft, smooth, wanton! hah, ah, ah! Ah Rogue, ah Rogue! here's shoulders, here's shape! there's a Foot and Leg, here's a Leg, here's a leg— Qua a-a-a-a.
    (Squeakes like a Cat, and tickles Beaugard's Legs.)
Courtine. What an old Goat's this!
Sir Jolly. Child, Child, Child, who's that? A friend of thine! a friend of thine? A pretty fellow, odd a very pretty fellow, and a strong dog I'll warrant him: how dost do dear heart? prithee let me kiss thee, I'll swear and vow I will kiss thee, ha, ha, ha, he, he, he a Toad, A Toad, ah Toa-a-a-ad—
Courtine. Sir, I am your humble Servant.
Beaugard. But the Lady, Sir *Jolly,* how does the Lady, what says the Lady, Sir *Jolly?*
Sir Jolly. What says the Lady! why she says—she says—odd she has a delicate Lip, such a Lip, so red, so hard, plump, so lub; I fancy I am eating Cherries every time I think on't—and for her Neck and Breasts and her—odds life; I'll say no more, not a word more, But I know, I know—

The Problem of Sympathy and Judgment

Beaugard. I am sorry for that with all my Heart; do you know, say you Sir, and would you put off your mumbled orts, your offall upon me?—
Sir Jolly. Hugh, hush, hush! have a care, as I live and breathe, not I, alack and well a day I am a poor fellow decay'd and done: Alls gone with me Gentlemen, but my good Nature; odd I love to know how matters go, though, now and then to see a pretty Wench and a young Fellow Towze and Rowze and Frouze and Mowze; odd I love a young fellow dearly, faith dearly—[4]

Sir Jolly—a pimp, a homosexual, a voyeur—explodes onto the stage in an avalanche of language, at once petulant, seductive, and demanding. Sir Jolly is not just a character; he is an event. When he is on stage, no character is safe. He completes his sentences either with exclamations or dashes, meaning that he has expressed either a very strong feeling or, through the trope that the schoolboys then called *aposiopesis,* he demands that the listener complete his thought. To the extent that the young soldiers—and the audience—complete his unfinished sentences, they are drawn into Sir Jolly's erotic vision and harebrained schemes. He directs the attention of the audience upward from Courtine's foot to his leg and then coyly stops; he directs their attention downward from Clarinda's lips to her neck and breasts but then coyly stops. Sir Jolly takes possession of the stage, and his thoughts become the focus—and focuser—of attention. As he conjures up wanton images for Beaugard, he invites the audience to experience the pleasures of voyeurism. Through his intensely visual imagery, he asks the audience to visualize a scene, to imagine further details that he suggests but does not state. As we complete the scene, we have been drawn into the voyeur's world of intensely *visualized* erotica.

The brief stage directions suggest how a talented actor like Leigh might enact Sir Jolly's style. Apparently Otway wanted the actor to look longingly at Beaugard's foot and leg and then tickle his legs. Sir Jolly's scream of delight probably coincides with his movement from foot to calf to thigh. Courtine, who likens Sir Jolly to an old goat, then becomes the object of Sir Jolly's fancy;

Sir Jolly's attempt to kiss him culminates in another scream of delight. During this frenzy Beaugard must repeat three times his request for information about Clarinda, each time being answered in progressively more suggestive visual imagery. Both seducer and pimp, Sir Jolly ceases his description at exactly the most suggestive moment. Both the audience and Beaugard get his "point," and Beaugard is alarmed that Sir Jolly should know such intimate details about Clarinda.[5] Affronted by Beaugard's suspicion, Sir Jolly confesses that he is always a spectator and never a participant: the peak of his pleasure is observation of towzing, rowzing, frowzing, and mowzing.[6] "This is the most extraordinary rogue," says Courtine, that he has ever seen. Indeed. From such an entrance, the audience should expect lively diversion from, if not direct involvement in, his erotic fantasies. Further, his manic style will make it difficult for other characters to predominate, reducing the seriousness of our concern with the cuckolding plot and the romantic subplot. While the audience may be titillated by the cuckolding plot and, like Sir Jolly, wish to see it carried to its conclusion, the audience should also recognize that it has been led by Sir Jolly, a clearly ridiculous character, to see the world through his eyes.

The Souldiers Fortune creates a comic world governed by grim irony, a world where expectation and result are never in accord. Who succeeds in this play? Who is rewarded? Sir Jolly never gets to see what he has schemed to arrange; Sir Davy fails to have Beaugard killed, but when he thinks he has succeeded, he fails to have Beaugard resurrected; Sir Davy fails to have Sir Jolly imprisoned for Beaugard's murder; Beaugard fails to win Clarinda's permanent affection; Clarinda is stuck with Sir Davy; the soldiers' fortune is not improved. Instances of irony could be multiplied, but the consistently ironic events suggest a world far from providential.[7] In such a world, what values are preserved and endorsed? Otway provides two tableaus of contemporary society, the first illustrating the deep corruption of society and the second indicating the importance of preserving simple virtues. I call these parts of the comedy "tableaus" because they are moral fables substituting for dramatic action. Near the middle

The Problem of Sympathy and Judgment

of the second act, Beaugard encounters Courtine, and both rail at "that moving lump of filthiness miscall'd a Man": a shabbily dressed military officer. The dumb show continues as the two ex-soldiers comment on a parade of symbols—the military, the Puritans, the law courts—that illustrate the hypocrisy and venality of society. Courtine notes, for example, that in civilian life the officer was a retailer of ale. He owes his rank to bribery of a colonel. Next Beaugard recalls the success with which a footman was raised to a high position because of aptitude for flattery, fawning, deceit, and espionage. In short, as Courtine grumbles, "'Tis as unreasonable to expect a man of Sense should be prefer'd, as 'tis to think a Hector can be stout, a Priest religious, a fair Woman chast, or a pardoned Rebel loyal" (p. 122).[8]

The rhetorical purpose of this panorama is to provide the generalizations about society to be tested specifically by the action of this comedy. In such a dismal world, Beaugard says, the only remaining virtues are friendship and drinking. At the beginning of the fourth act, Otway presents a more positive vision.

Beaugard. Ah *Courtine!* must we be always idle? must we never see our glorious days again? when shall we be rowling in the Lands of Milk and Honey; incampt in large luxuriant Vineyards, where the loadded vines Cluster about our Tents, drink the rich Juice, just prest from the plump Grape, feeding on all the fragrant golden Fruit that grow in fertile Climes, and ripen'd by the earliest vigour of the Sun?

Courtine. Ah *Beaugard!* those days have been, but now we must resolve to content our selves at an humble rate: me thinks it is not unpleasant to consider how I have seen thee in a large Pavillion; drowning the heat of the day in *Campagne* Wines, sparkling sweet as those charmed Beauties, whose dear remembrance every glass recorded, with half a dozen honest Fellows more; Friends, *Beaugard*, faithful hearty Friends, things as hard to meet with as preferment here: Fellows that would speak truth boldly, and were proud on'it, that scorn'd flattery, loved honesty, for 'twas their portion, and never yet learn'd the Trade of ease and lying. (p. 151)

Such nostalgic dialogue, a substitute for action, presents a tableau of human relationships that contrasts sharply with those of the earlier tableau. Presented in the second and fourth acts, the tableaus juxtapose images of corruption with images of harmonious male friendship. These tableaus allow Otway to place the specific concerns of *The Souldiers Fortune* within the context of a larger world of ethical principles and social problems. In Otway's world, corruption in the military and the law reflect and reinforce the corruption latent in other human relationships.[9] Love relationships are not safe, as the sad experience of Beaugard and Clarinda signifies. And while love apparently promises happiness for Courtine and Sylvia, the promise is hollow. Early in this play, Sylvia commiserates with Clarinda about the ugliness of unhappy marriage, saying that it would be "an unspeakable blessing to lye all night by a Horse-load of diseases; a beastly, unsavory, old, groaning, grunting, wheazing Wretch, that smells of the Grave he's going to already; from such a curse and Hair-Cloath next my skin good Heaven deliver me!" (p. 107).

Yet in *The Atheist,* which shows Courtine and Sylvia after one year of marriage, Sylvia speaks thus of her spouse:

> *A Husband's . . . like his Wedding-Clothes,*
> *Worn gay a Weak, but then he throws 'em off,*
> *And With 'em too the Lover: Then his Days*
> *Grow gay abroad, and his Nights dull at home:*
> *He lies whole Months by thy poor longing Side*
> *Heavy and useless, comes faint and loth to Bed,*
> *Turns him about, grunts, snores: and that's a Husband.*
>
> (p. 340)

And if the bride's blank verse makes her sound a bit like a tragic heroine, Courtine has an even less flattering definition of wife:

> I am forced to call a Woman I do not like, by the name of Wife; and lie with her, for the most part, with no Appetite at all; must keep the Children that, for ought I know, any Body else may beget of her Body; and for Food and Rayment, by her good will she would have them both Fresh three times a day: Then for Kiss and part, I may kiss my Heart out, but the Devil a bit shall I ever get rid of her. . . . By the

The Problem of Sympathy and Judgment

vertue of Matrimony and long Cohabitation, we are grown so really One Flesh, that I have no more Inclination to hers, than to eat a piece of my own.... In short, *Jack,* she has so order'd the Bus'ness, that I am half weary of the World, wish all Mankind hang'd, and have not laugh'd these Six months (p. 305).

So much for marriage as a refuge from the corruption of the world.

While it may not be entirely fair to use *The Atheist* as a commentary on *The Souldiers Fortune,* it would be foolish to ignore that Beaugard, Courtine, and Sylvia appear in a comedy produced only two years later and subtitled "the second part" of *The Souldiers Fortune. The Atheist* extends and darkens the pessimism introduced in *The Souldiers Fortune.* Although the comedy has some terribly funny scenes (e.g., the resurrection of Beaugard, Bloody Bones's ghoulish appetite, Sir Davy and the ghost, and others), such scenes do little to lighten the tone. It is not accidental that the last half of the play occurs at night.[10] In the fifth act, Otway must resolve the problems he has introduced, and he will do this under cover of darkness. To Sylvia and Courtine, Otway promises marriage. But the reaction of other characters to their marriage is a significant omen. Sir Jolly is as antimatrimonial as one would expect from his earlier pronouncements. "I don't like these Marriages, I'll have no Marriages in my House, and there's an end on't" (p. 193). But Sir Davy's reaction is totally unexpected: he affirms the marriage in hysterical glee. It is difficult to imagine how Otway wanted Mr. Nokes to exhibit Sir Davy in the fifth act. When he learns of Sylvia's elopement, he responds with *apparent* pleasure. "With all my heart, I am glad on't Child, I would not care if [Courtine] had carry'd away my House and all, Man; unhappy news quotha! poor Fool, he does not know I am a Cuckold, and that any body may make bold with what belongs to me, ha, ha, ha; I am so pleas'd, ha, ha, ha. I think I was never so pleas'd in all my life before, ha, ha, ha" (p. 192).

In each of his remaining four speeches Sir Davy utters the same laugh and strikes the same self-congratulatory stance: he laughs as he makes his peace with Lady Dunce and Beaugard.

Even paying a dowry of 5,000 pounds does not disturb him. Furthermore, he agrees to Beaugard's "covenants of Performance" as part of reconciliation to Beaugard. At best, Sir Davy's forced laughter suggests his hysterical tension is dissipating: as dawn approaches and the ghost dissolves, he loses his terror. At worst, he is now deranged and finds all misfortune risible. To be sure, he flashes a little wit in his benediction on Sylvia's marriage, saying to Courtine, "Here, take thy Bride, like Man and Wife agree,/And may she prove as true—as mine to me" (p. 193). But the most likely way for an actor to play Sir Davy would be to indicate despair behind his manic laughter. He is as dislocated as the young soldiers at the beginning of the play: fortune, indeed, has been cruel. Clarinda is in the same miserable condition at the end of the play as at the beginning. The young soldiers are no closer to status or security than in the first scene. The only unalloyed values that Otway offers are the images of male friendship and of drinking. These values, celebrated in nostalgic reflections but not in dramatic action, seem durable, but they are useful in this comic world only as foils to the corrupt relationships exhibited among the characters.

Thus, *The Atheist* deepens and refines the comic vision introduced in *The Souldiers Fortune*. Otway significantly complicates the issue of marriage, focusing not on the misery of enforced marriage—though that theme is present (p. 182)—but of bad marriage itself. Husband and wife are equally unhappy and equally trapped in their unhappiness. While *The Souldiers Fortune* extends the possibility of romantic love as an alternative to oppressive marriage, *The Atheist* dashes that hope.[11] Beaugard's marriage to Porcia at the end of *The Atheist* ignores and does not resolve the marital problems central to these two comedies. Otway's comic vision does not affirm the marriages that the endings of his comedies seem to celebrate.

If Otway offers a comic world from which there is no exit, Shadwell offers a choice of exits that lead only to dead ends. First staged at Drury Lane in May 1688, *The Squire of Alsatia* was immediately successful and continued to be staged for a half century. Through the epigraph taken from Horace's *Epistle to*

The Problem of Sympathy and Judgment

Augustus, Shadwell laments the taste of the present age, a theme he develops in the epilogue by presenting a "history" of English drama from 1660 to 1688. First, he says, were the rhymed plays, followed by "Ranting Fustian" and then by "the vile Usurper Farce." Then came spectacle. But now Shadwell offers a true comedy.

> *If all this stuff has not quite spoyl'd your taste,*
> *Pray let a Comedy once more be grac'd*
> *Which does not Monsters represent, but men,*
> *Conforming to the Rules of Master Ben.*
> *Our Author, ever having him in view,*
> *At humble distance would his steps pursue.*
> *He to correct, and to inform did write:*
> *If Poets aim at nought but to delight,*
> *Fidlers have to the Bays an equal right.*[12]

Despite Shadwell's claims to moral edification, Nicoll denounced this play as "hopelessly and permeatingly vulgar, brutal, and immoral."[13] Arthur H. Scouten and Robert D. Hume, far from accepting Nicoll's judgment, argue that *The Squire of Alsatia* signals "the rise of the 'new' style in comedy. . . . Double entendre Shadwell does indeed avoid, but his hero, Belfond Jr., seduces, abandons, and pays off a basically virtuous girl in the course of the play. We learn also that he has a child by another mistress. And yet Shadwell loudly trumpets the young man's reform, and explicitly holds him up as a model gentleman."[14] While I believe that the position of Scouten and Hume is more nearly correct than Nicoll's, several important critical questions are by no means solved. If the "key" to the comedy is Belfond's reform, then we must take the reform seriously. Can we? And if his reform is not believable, how are we to regard the play? Forgetting for the moment the long succession of later comedies in which reform *is* taken seriously, how are we to understand the values endorsed in *The Squire of Alsatia?* How does Shadwell structure plot and character to communicate his comic vision?

Shadwell's comedy emerges from and exploits the contrasts and conflicts between three groups of characters. Significantly,

Belfond Junior is a member of each group. The elder brothers, Sir William and Sir Edward Belfond, disagree about the proper way to raise young men.[15] Belfond Senior and Belfond Junior represent different styles of young men in London and are the young men whose education is debated by Sir William and Sir Edward. Finally, three young women (Termagant, Lucia, and Isabella) represent three different claims on Belfond Junior: Termagant is the cast-off mistress; Lucia is the naïf whose status is unclear until the end of the play; and Isabella is the wealthy young woman whose virtue, beauty, and wealth will lead Belfond Junior to the altar. Other contrasts (e.g., country life vs. city life) overlay these contrasts and conflicts, and Shadwell is careful to sustain and heighten them until the final scene. Seemingly at the heart of the play is the issue of what kind of adult behavior Shadwell endorses, his notion of the gentleman. But Shadwell has altered his Roman source, Terence's *The Brothers,* to such an extent that Shadwell's vision is at once more complex and more difficult to describe than Terence's.[16] By changing the role of young women in the play, Shadwell has greatly complicated his vision, which at first appears to be rooted in the debate between Sir William and Sir Edward.

Near the end of the first act, Sir William and Sir Edward Belfond debate conflicting philosophies of raising children and, by implication, different philosophies of human nature and standards of adult conduct. While their argument initially seems to be about the boy that each man has raised, their argument is framed in sufficiently general terms that the play may "settle" both the general and the specific debate. To put it another way, the debate is elaborated so tendentiously in the first, third, and fifth acts that the audience expects a decisive answer to a simple question: which brother is correct? The general lines of the argument are introduced at the end of the first act as they discuss the moral probity of Belfond Junior.

Sir Edward. . . . Nay there you wrong him; he does no ungentlemanlike things: Prithee consider *Youth* a little: What if he does Wench a little and now and then is somewhat

The Problem of Sympathy and Judgment

> extravagant in Wine? Where is the great Crime: All young fellows that have mettle in them will do the first; and if they have wit and good humour in them, in this drinking Country, they will sometimes be forc'd upon the latter; and he must be a very dull phlematick Lump, whom Wine will not elevate to some Extravagance now and then. . . .
>
> *Sir William.* . . . How can he be reclaim'd without severity? . . . Cudgel him, and allow him no Mony; make him not dare to offend you thus. Well, I have a Son whom by my strictness I have form'd according to my heart; He never puts on his Hat in my presence; Rises at second Course, takes away his Plate, says Grace, and saves me the Charge of a Chaplain. When ever he committed a fault, I maul'd him with Correction; I'd fain see him once dare to be extravagant; No, he's a good Youth, the Comfort of my Age; I weep for joy to think of him. . . .
>
> *Sir Edward.* . . . Too much streightness to the minds of Youths, like too much lacing to the Body, will make them grow Crooked.
>
> *Sir William.* But no lacing at all, will make them swell and grow Monsters. (P. 220)

With the debate introduced in the first act, Shadwell develops and partially resolves the issue by using the young brothers as "test cases" for each father's philosophy. In doing so, however, Shadwell dramatizes cases that cut both ways, in effect partially supporting and partially undercutting each father's position.

If the focus in Terence is the older brothers, then a major shift in Shadwell's version is the preeminence of the younger brothers. The argument between Sir William and Sir Edward provides an intellectual framework for the play, but the plot hinges on two intrigues: the rebellious attempt of Belfond Senior to become a "gentleman" and the attempt of Belfond Junior to manage his romantic escapades. The Alsatian bullies dominate Belfond Senior because of his intense rebellion against his father's Spartan values: "Well, I'll endur't no longer! If I can but raise Money," he snarls in the opening scene, "I'll teach him to use his Son like a Dog, I'll warrant him" (p. 210). Even Lolpoop, the bumptious, rustic servant, sees more clearly than his master: "Ods-flesh, I'll dye the Death of a Dog, and aw these yeow seen here, be not Rogues, Cheats, and Pickpockets" (p. 215). But his perceptions and counsel are disregarded. Shadwell thus insists that our opening view of Belfond Senior be very negative and that the dispute between the older brothers is initially tipped in Sir Edward's favor. Indeed, since the audience sees the loutish, vain Belfond Senior before it hears the debate, the audience is predisposed to accept Sir Edward's position. Belfond Senior is clearly not evidence that Sir William's philosophy is successful. Ignorant of Belfond Senior's rebellion but confident that each knows the character of Belfond Junior, the older brothers decide to settle their debate by examining the conduct of Belfond Junior. If the young man is with a good author—rather than with a whore—then the debate, say the brothers, will be settled conclusively. In the next act Shadwell introduces a wealth of evidence, but neither position is conclusively supported.

In the second act Shadwell moves from the abstract terms of the debate to the specific case, showing the audience Belfond Junior in his bedroom. Engaged neither in study nor in romance, Belfond Junior is comforting Lucia, whom he has seduced and who now fears herself pregnant. If anything, seducing a "virtuous" young woman might be considered worse than consorting with a whore. Shadwell develops the scene ambiguously, arousing considerable sympathy for Lucia and portraying Belfond Junior as a cad.

To the disconsolate young woman, Belfond Junior maintains that she should not despair because she has done "no more than [her] whole Sex is born to do" (p. 222). She should not feel undone, he says, for "thou art made: Woman is but half a Creature, till she be joyn'd to Man; now thou art whole and perfect" (p. 223). His replies might seem very amusing raillery if not for Lucia's presence—and the severity of her distress. In Terence, Pamphila, the pregnant young woman, is not developed extensively but the young man does marry her; in Shadwell, Lucia makes several appearances and is a thoroughly decent, naïve young woman, one trapped in a complex social dilemma. She is not a comic butt, and her innocence is pathetic. Having introduced her, Shadwell then has her hide in Belfond Junior's

The Problem of Sympathy and Judgment

closet—a staple device of concealment—so she is not seen by Belfond Junior's singing master nor his friend Truman. From this vantage point, though, both she—and the audience—share the young men's table talk. What must Lucia think about Belfond Junior—and her own situation—when Belfond Junior assures Truman that carnal appetites will always overthrow Honesty and Morality, so he need not worry about being a sincere, honest lover (p. 225)? What must she—and the audience—think when Truman reports on the assignation he is arranging for them with two women who are closely guarded because one has been promised to Belfond Senior? Her musings are interrupted by the first of Termagant's six violent appearances.[17] Belfond Junior tells Termagant, who has had a child by him, that when he is done with a woman, she is fit for all mankind (p. 277). But at the sound of another visitor's arrival, Termagant also hides in the closet.

The thought of two persons hiding in the same closet—especially two women who love or loved the same man—is inherently comic, and so the audience waits in anticipation of their eruption from the closet. What the audience has learned thus far about Belfond Junior is far from positive. Hume argues that "Shadwell is showing the maturation process of a virtuous and honorable young man. He certainly does not regard Belfond Jr. as a rake, or consider his conduct reprehensible."[18] But given the immediacy of the young man's predicament—his affection for Lucia and his contempt for Termagant have been dramatized—the audience can hardly be expected to wink approvingly. If Belfond Senior is an indictment of Sir William's philosophy, then Belfond Junior cannot, at this point, be regarded as vindication of Sir Edward's.

The third set of visitors, Sir Edward and Sir William, specifically ask Belfond Junior whether he has been with a whore. Belfond Junior swears not only that he will not lie but that Sir William's suspicions are entirely unwarranted. Of course the young man has lied twice: he has lied about lying; and he has also lied about his sexual adventures. Having given this answer, Shadwell provides an immediate judgment of the answer by having Lucia and Termagant spill into the room. Caught in the first two of several critical lies, Belfond Junior lies once more about Lucia's status, claiming she is a servant, but confesses that Termagant is a discarded mistress. Out of respect for the delicacy of Lucia's status, his lie may seem excusable, but he does not justify it at the time in an aside as he does in two later scenes (pp. 252 and 275), where he indicates to the audience that he is lying deliberately. The audience, like Lucia, surely sees Belfond's duplicity as well as his profligacy. But how harshly does she—and should the audience—judge him? Sir William's obloquy is as immoderate as we would expect, for he is gratified to find his prejudices supported; Sir Edward is not convinced that his son has been licentious. But one scene does not settle the debate, and having introduced both younger brothers, Shadwell further complicates the contrary claims of sympathy and judgment.

Shadwell concludes the second act by giving the audience yet another chance to compare the younger brothers. Dressed and coached by Hackum, Shamwell, and other Alsatian exiles, Belfond Senior declares himself the paragon of civilized life: "my father kept me in ignorance, and would have made a very silly Blockheadly *Put* of me; Why I never heard a Gentleman Banter, or cut a Sham in my life before" (p. 233). Instead, his rural curriculum had included farming, drinking, driving a hard bargain, carpentry and bricklaying, and traveling over the estate (p. 232). Resplendent with a new patois and expensive finery, he is too drunk to speak to Sir William, who is taunted and finally driven away by the Alsatian rabble. By the end of this act, the audience must wonder whether either philosophy of education is commendable. While each of the older brothers believes that only his approach has merit, neither of the younger brothers seems exemplary proof. Just as Belfond Senior is ensnared in the life of a seamy group, Belfond Junior seems caught in rather complex romantic attachments. Through carefully structuring the conflict and contrast between both sets of brothers in the first two acts, Shadwell can refine and extend the debate in the last half of the play.

At the opening of the third act, Sir Edward advises Belfond

The Problem of Sympathy and Judgment

Junior about the wages of sin. "There's nothing but Anxiety in Vice," he confides. "I am not streight Lac'd; but when I was Young, I ne'r knew any thing gotten by Wenching, but Duels, Claps, and Bastards: And every drunken fit is a short madness, that cuts off a good part of Life" (p. 238). Belfond Junior is no stranger to "Anxiety in Vice," though Sir Edward knows less of his story than the audience does. However natural wenching may be to young men, it inevitably complicates their lives in unhappy ways, says Sir Edward. And to accentuate the point, Shadwell brings in Termagant just before and just after Sir Edward's avuncular advice. In her second visit, she pursues Lucia, threatening to slit her nose and then to cut her up and bake her in a pie for Belfond Junior (p. 240). Anxiety in vice, indeed, is not restricted to young men.

Sir Edward's counsel considered not only wenching but drunkenness, and Shadwell illustrates the "anxiety" caused by this vice later when Belfond Senior, thoroughly drunk, is being groomed for marriage to Termagant (p. 242). Belfond Junior immediately recognizes his brother's companions for the scoundrels they are; but he has much trouble convincing his brother to "see" them as Alsatian bullies rather than as fine wits.[19] The dispute over vision echoes the dispute between the older brothers: stated simply, none of the brothers, older or younger, is willing to revise his judgments in light of the evidence; each wants only to find more evidence to fortify his position. Of the four, Sir William and his son Belfond Senior are most benighted; but Sir Edward and Belfond Junior have the problem only to a slighter degree. When Belfond Junior leads Hackum by the nose to illustrate his cowardice, Belfond Senior sees Hackum's meekness as evidence of loyalty to him. When Belfond Junior kicks Cheatly and Shamwell, they reply that their sense of honor and breeding make them pacific (p. 246).

The third act concludes by further complicating the attitude of the audience toward Lucia and, by implication, toward Belfond Junior. The last two scenes invite special contrast between Lucia and the two beauties sought by Truman and Belfond Junior, for both scenes deal with the relation of daughters (or nieces) to fathers (or uncles). Lucia's father, an attorney, is dismayed by the lurid story that Termagant weaves (p. 248). Lucia denies Termagant's story three times, but her father—an entirely good and decent man—disbelieves her and sends her home, sure that news of her seduction and pregnancy will kill her mother. "Have I besto'd so much, and taken so much care in thy education," he cries, "to have no other Fruit but this?" (p. 248). Once more Shadwell demands that the audience see the very real human pain caused by seduction and abandonment—the anxiety in vice—as well as pregnancy out of wedlock. Shadwell's emphasis on the pathos of Lucia's predicament—an emphasis not found in his source—contrasts with his treatment of Termagant, who is so spectacularly shrewish and fiendishly wicked that she seems to deserve her shabby treatment, if not worse. No such case can be made against Lucia.

In contrast to Termagant and Lucia, Teresia and Isabella are innocents eager for adventure. Chafing under the supervision of a strict father/uncle (Scrapeall), who has forbidden dancing, singing, and nonreligious conversation, the women are fomenting rebellion. Scrapeall is introduced in the first act as an excessively pious, psalm-singing scrivener—contemporary codewords for a canting hypocrite at best, a greedy scoundrel at worst (p. 217). Like a *senex amans*, the iron-fisted guardian invites rebellion if his wards are high-spirited. As the third act ends, Shadwell has introduced and developed conflicts between four sets of parents and children, conflicts in whose resolution Belfond Junior will play some role. Scrapeall has been a tyrant and will certainly be "punished" for this; Lucia's father has been a lenient father, from what we have seen, but he has not been "rewarded," and his suffering seems heartfelt. Sir William has been a tyrant but has not been punished yet; Sir Edward has been a lenient father, but he has not seen his son mature into a real gentleman. Since Belfond Junior plays a significant role in freeing Isabella from Scrapeall and in reconciling the other parents and children (Lucia and her father, Belfond Senior and Sir William), his development in the final acts is crucial to Shadwell's comic vision and to his statement about raising children. Basically, Shadwell has three options for him: let him remain a rake, confirmed in vice; let him "reform," freed from anxiety; or let him remain at the end as he is in the beginning, a basically good-natured young man more anxious to please his father than to avoid vice.

Like the second act, the fourth act opens with Belfond Junior once more consoling Lucia. Lucia says that if he really loved her—a promise he made earlier and will repeat moments after—he would abandon the whole world. "Thou hast so kindly oblig'd me, I shall never never cease to love thee," he replies (p. 252). Forgetting her own dilemma, she swoons, blissfully convinced of Belfond Junior's fidelity. The audience must certainly find his aside disquieting. "Now here's a mischief on the other side; For how can a good natur'd man think of ever quitting so tender, and so kind a Mistress, whom no respect, but Love has thrown into my Arms: And yet I must: But I will better her condition" (p. 252). Belfond's duplicity parallels his lies to Lucia in the second act, and in fact this scene grimly echoes the earlier in other important ways: once more Truman ends the scene by coming to Belfond's chambers; once more he has come to report on his progress with Teresia and Isabella. Once more the audience sympathizes with Lucia and censures her lover. In defense of Belfond, I should note that he claims to have taken care of Termagant, and he promises—even if in an aside—to take care of Lucia, too. But since the expense will be borne by Sir Edward, Belfond's "reform" is in no way demonstrated. His callousness, moreover, raises serious questions about the high esteem in which Sir Edward, a good man, holds him. To the extent that the audience sympathizes with Lucia, they judge him more harshly.

As Sir William, Sir Edward, and Scrapeall discuss the suitability of Isabella for Belfond Senior, Sir William explodes once more at his brother's undue concern for the young people's mutual affection. "He like her! What's matter whether he like her, or no? Is it not enough for him, that I do? Is a Son, a Boy, a Jackanapes, to have a will of his own? That were to have him be the Father, and me the Son" (p. 253). Sir William's callous disregard for his son's feelings is sharply contrasted with the melancholy appearance of Lucia's father (p. 255), grieving over his daughter's seduction. Sir William is delighted by Sir Edward's willingness to "take care of" Lucia, for he sees it as admission of his brother's failure. He is convinced that the debate has been settled in his favor. But Sir William's glee is brief, for he sees Lolpoop, the servant of Belfond Senior, promenading with a whore, and learns that his son is no longer in the country. The connection between the two events is unmistakable, and Sir William is deranged, repeating the violent pattern of action in the second act. Once more Sir William is at the center of a riot. When Sir William confronts his son, Belfond Senior seethes and even growls a bit but can only say, "bow wow," ironically confirming his initial characterization of himself as his father's dog (p. 263). Brandishing his new cant like a sword, Belfond distances himself from his tyrannical father, who is swarmed over by the rabble but saved by Belfond Junior. At this point Sir William can admit his blindness about Belfond Senior, whom he derides as a "most ungracious Rebel, that Monster of Villany" (p. 267), but this admission does not settle the debate central to the play. Is Belfond Senior really a monster, or is this judgment as immoderate and wrongheaded as his earlier judgments of his two sons? Is his judgment Shadwell's judgment?

The final act opens with two groups, freshly penitent, defending themselves. The Alsatian bullies, punished ignominiously by the authorities, complain of ill use and vow revenge. Belfond Junior pleads his case to Scrapeall. Just as the Alsatian bullies want revenge on Sir William (and therefore plan to wed Belfond Senior to Termagant at once), Belfond Junior wants revenge on Termagant. He wails, "Was ever man plagu'd with a Wench like me? Well, say what they will, the life of a Whore-master is a foolish, restless, anxious life" (p. 269). Clearly, Belfond Junior accepts Sir Edward's position on wenching, and it now would seem that he is well on the way to reformation, making *The Squire of Alsatia* an example of comic fare that would dominate the stage about a decade later.[20] Whether the reform is meant to be "straight" is a more complex question. Richard Levin argues incisively against the methodological assumptions of critics who discover "ironic" readings in almost every Renaissance play.[21] His argument carries equal force in evaluating ironic readings of Restoration comedies. Nevertheless, the audience must wonder about the depth of Belfond Junior's reform when he swears to Isabella, "I never was yet contracted to any Woman, nor made the least promise, or give any one the least hope of it; and if I do not demonstrate my innocence to you, I will be content for ever to be debarr'd the sight of you, more priz'd by me than Liberty, or Life" (p. 270). Clearly, Belfond Junior has lied: these protestations are insincere, or his protestations to Lucia were insincere, or his protestations to both women were sincere but he is highly fickle. None of these possibilities makes Belfond Junior especially attractive or his reform very convincing. By introducing both Termagant and Lucia, Shadwell avoids easy affirmations about marriage and a platitudinous ending in which all the "good" characters are rewarded and all the bad characters punished.

Belfond Junior's lie to Lucia's father—that Lucia is innocent—initially seems commendable. In an aside, he remarks, "If a Lie be ever lawful, 'tis in this case." But the lie is gratuitous and untimely. The facts of Lucia's condition have been established by Termagant's report; the parents' grief has been cited twice; Lucia's father is an attorney and thus may be more astute than others at discriminating between hearsay and fact. The attorney's demeanor and his acceptance of Sir Edward's generous settlement suggest how silly Belfond Junior's lie must seem to him. This final lie is not inconsistent with Shadwell's characterization of him as a young man of basically good nature who simply cannot tell the truth.

Having saved Belfond Senior from marriage to Termagant, Belfond Junior is thus instrumental in uniting his brother and Sir William. But the reconciliation of fathers and sons and the union of Belfond Junior and Isabella are complicated by the recurrence of old errors. Having abandoned his Draconian style, Sir William again embraces the opposite extreme. Sir William not only forgives Belfond Senior for his excesses; he will "let him spend what he will, I'll come up to London, Feast and Revel, and never take a Minutes care while I Breath again" (p. 276). Sir William glosses this position a little later by saying, "all Human Care is vain" (p. 278). Is this the lesson to be learned from his misadventure? Belfond Senior vows to have his fling at whoring before he marries (p. 279), presumably with his father's blessing. Is this the stance that Shadwell endorses, or is this not another instance of one extreme position replacing another? Isabella is understandably concerned about the reliability of her future husband after seeing his family's reunion and watching Sir Edward tidy up some very loose ends: Shadwell satisfies Isabella's concerns with the weakest kinds of support.

Isabella. How can *I* be secure you will not fall to your old courses agen?
Belfond Junior. *I* have been so sincere in my Confessions, you may trust me; but *I* call Heav'n to witness, *I* will hereafter be entirely yours. *I* look on Marriage as the most solemn Vow a Man can make; and 'tis by consequence, the basest Perjury to break it.
Ruth. Come, come, I know your mind, too, take him, take him.
Isabella. If Fate will have it so. (P. 280)

On one hand, what else could Belfond Junior say to convince Isabella? On the other hand, he has pledged constancy too often for his final pledge to ring true.

The Squire of Alsatia "works" if Belfond Junior's reform is convincing. Shadwell presents him as a character with many positive features: wit, courage, and devotion to his father. But he is singularly unsuccessful at managing his romantic life, and his pattern of deception-under-pressure surely works to his discredit. Shadwell complicates Terence by introducing two women of opposite dispositions but with similar claims on Belfond Junior. Shadwell's "solution" is only a partial solution but points the way for other dramatists to exploit the "reform" plot more convincingly. In light of the significant changes Shadwell has made in his

The Problem of Sympathy and Judgment

source, his comic vision is not precisely reflected in the moral tags offered at the end by Belfond Junior ("There is no peace but in a Virtuous Life./Nor lasting Joy but in a tender Wife") or Sir Edward ("Severity spoils ten, for one it mends;/If you'd not have your Sons desire your ends,/By Gentleness and Bounty make those Sons your Friends"). Neither maxim has been tested in this comedy. Certainly the play does consider—and evaluate— two philosophies of raising children, but its paean to virtue and fidelity is unsupported by the dramatic action.

Shadwell's promise in the prologue to follow Jonson is not what he delivers. What Shadwell claims to say and what the play "says" are quite different. The grim reality of Termagant's situation (in the final act, we learn that Belfond Junior has kidnapped her child to keep her at bay) and the obvious pathos of Lucia and her father make Belfond Junior's reform necessary but not necessarily convincing. Both characters are developed too attractively and too vividly for the audience to dismiss them as literary conventions. If Shadwell had wanted to produce a thoroughly convincing reform comedy, then he has failed. Sir Edward never discovers the extent of Belfond Junior's deception; Sir William goes from one extreme position to another; Belfond Senior is not likely to become a true gentleman and is a very long way from understanding the "anxiety in vice" described by Sir Edward and Belfond Junior. Belfond Junior marries his heiress, pledging constancy as he had at the beginning of the second and fourth acts to another woman. Shadwell has structured a comedy around a series of contrasts, leading the audience both to sympathize with and judge his major characters. His vision is not found in the statements of any of his characters but grows out of the pattern of action so carefully developed. Though it is tempting to see *The Squire of Alsatia* either as a comedy that endorses debauchery or proclaims moral reform, the comedy cannot be both nor convincingly be interpreted in either way. Shadwell has given the audience several sets of "opposites," but he does not finally endorse any of the extreme positions represented by Sir Edward and Lucia's father or by Sir William and Scrapeall. If

Shadwell sees a fail-proof strategy for raising children—the particular ethical concern in this play—he does not disclose it. His comedy dramatizes various unsuccessful strategies, and given the complications he introduces, the conclusion seems more optimistic than it is. That the play has been read by critics who see it as a "reform" comedy or as an example of debauchery takes this study back to the heart of the critical questions that underlie this study and animate the *moralisé* tradition.

Any reader of the criticism of Restoration comedy must be struck by its critics' uncommonly sharp disagreements and the rather spectacular changes in fortune enjoyed by some authors and plays during the last three centuries. But the perdurable faith that the comedies, or at least most of them, are "moral" remains as unshaken as it is unproven, though the notions of what "moral" refers to have shifted a great deal during the same time. Future critics will have the benefit of more historical knowledge about the theater and the economic, political, and literary constraints that affected repertory companies and authors in the late seventeenth century.[22] These critics will know more about the audiences of the Restoration theatre[23] and about the ways in which those audiences may have responded to plays.[24] Articles, monographs, and books on individual authors or kinds of plays will no doubt sharpen the sensitivity of future critics to important distinctions or nuances of meaning that have thus far been inadequately interpreted. But whatever the advantages of future critics, they will not necessarily have easy answers to some questions central to the present study.

First, the question of "instruction" has not been conclusively settled. Hume has reviewed theories of comedy during the Restoration and has clearly presented the widely held beliefs about how comedy "teaches," or, more precisely, how different kinds of comedies achieve different kinds of effects.[25] The question of "instruction" really asks about the meaning of a literary work. In dealing with comedies, one could easily inquire into the differences in meaning, say, between reading a play and watching a performance of it. The printed text and the performed text may

The Problem of Sympathy and Judgment

differ widely in "meaning," but very little criticism has investigated this issue. Shadwell, Wycherley, and Otway wrote for the live theatre, meaning that they were interested in theatrical success and financial reward. How their work was regarded was in part determined by what other plays were being offered that season or had been successful in recent seasons. Moreover, the skill of actresses and actors no doubt affected the reception of plays, both new and old. In enacting a text, the cast was committed to an interpretation of the meaning of the text. Where modern critics can argue about the *real* meaning of *The Country Wife* and have found at least a dozen *real* meanings, Messrs. Hart, Mohun, Lydal, and others could only present one interpretation at a time.[26] Given Shadwell's claim that *The Squire of Alsatia* offered more than "mere" entertainment, what did his play mean (or "say" or "teach") in the 1680s? What might it mean in performance on PBS in central Pennsylvania in 1981? Literary critics often seem unaware that plays are not novels or lyric poetry, incapable of being studied in the same way and with the same methodological assumptions about "meaning" appropriate for other kinds of literature.

Aside from the intrinsic value of understanding the answer to this richly complex question, the critics should realize that the belief in the *moralisé* tradition is part of a larger network of beliefs about the nature, function, and enduring value of the humanities. The National Endowment for the Humanities, departments of literature, cadres of humanists in other departments or professional associations—their existence reflects in part the belief that reading great literature is somehow "good" for the audience, "good" in ways that have thus far not been fully understood. Though professional readers may disagree about which works of literature are great, they undoubtedly believe, perhaps uncritically, that reading great works of literature is sufficiently "good" or "valuable" that public funds ought to be allocated to foster further reading and study of those works. As I argued in chapter four, humanists have a litany of claims about the effects of imaginative literature, and if the argument from tradition or authority were convincing, then the question would be settled. But humanists have thus far adduced no arguments for or analyses of literary instruction that go much beyond introspection, anecdote, and a priori claims.

Social scientists, studying forms of literature that at best are marginal (e.g., pornographic films or stories and "violent" films or stories), have not found conclusive evidence that imaginative literature has any lasting effects or that exposure to imaginative literature is likely to benefit—or harm—its audience. Indeed, few humanists have speculated on the significance of a recent murder trial in Florida, a case where defense attorneys for a teenage murderer, Danny Zamora, argued that the defendant had committed the crime because of "television intoxication." The essence of their argument, which was supported by several social scientists and disputed by others, was that extensive exposure to literature (in this case, whatever shows he watched) had a pernicious effect on the defendant, leading him to commit a violent crime. The defense attorneys' argument echoes the argument of Jeremy Collier about Restoration comedies, works of literature that he read but never saw on stage. And Collier echoes Plato. The quarrel about the relation of literature and morality is an ancient one, one that is too important for humanists to ignore with impunity.

Such questions as the effects of literature on various audiences can be investigated with sophistication and discernment by humanists knowledgeable about empirical methods of research. Notwithstanding David Bleich's objections, such research is capable of confirming whether some important claims about literature are verifiable. But at present few humanists are working in this area of criticism, and what work that is done reflects the interests of social psychologists and sociologists rather than those of literary critics. This lacuna is serious but remediable.

All research is potentially revolutionary because its results may threaten established beliefs and structures or groups that depend on the validity of those beliefs for their purpose. Humanists must admit at least the possibility that imaginative literature does not predictably provide "instruction" as traditionally understood or does not appreciably affect its audience. Such a finding would not imply that literature is not "good" or valuable or important or worth teaching and preserving as important parts of our culture. It would, however, force humanists to articulate other, more compelling reasons for studying literature and refocus their discussion of how literature achieves its effects and communicates visions of life not possible in any other medium.

Notes
Selected Bibliography
Index

Notes

Preface
1. F. W. Bateson, "Second Thoughts: II. L. C. Knights and Restoration Comedy," *EIC*, 7 (1957), 67.
2. George Santayana, *Reason in Art* (New York: Scribner's, 1905), p. 168.
3. *Restoration Dramatists: A Collection of Critical Essays* (Englewood Cliffs, N.J.: Prentice-Hall, 1966), pp. 2–3.
4. *A History of Restoration Drama, 1660–1700*, 4th ed., Vol. I of *A History of English Drama, 1660–1900* (Cambridge: Cambridge Univ. Press, 1952), pp. 193–201. The 1923 edition contains the same information.
5. See Robert D. Hume, "Diversity and Development in Restoration Comedy, 1660–1679," *Eighteenth-Century Studies* (Spring 1972), 365–97, and A. H. Scouten, "Notes Toward a History of Restoration Comedy," *PQ*, 45 (1966), 62–70. See especially Hume's definitive study, *The Development of English Drama in the Late Seventeenth Century* (Oxford: Clarendon Press, 1976), pp. 63–126.
6. *The World We Have Lost* (New York: Scribner's, 1966). Laslett's study is a useful corrective for many of the "received truths" about the past (e.g., in the Renaissance many women married in their early teens as Shakespeare's Juliet does).
7. "Literature No 'Document'" *MLR*, 19 (1924), 143. See also his "'Real Society' in Restoration Comedy," *MLN*, 58 (1943), 175–81, and "The *Beau Monde* at the Restoration," *MLN*, 49 (1934), 425–32.

Chapter 1. "This lubrique and adult'rate age": The Attacks on Restoration Comedy
1. *A Short View* (London, 1698), p. 1. Hereafter cited parenthetically.
2. *Lives of the Poets*, ed. George Birkbeck Hill, 3 vols. (New York: Octagon Books, 1967), II, 222.

Notes to Pages 1–12

3. Thomas Babington Macaulay, "Comic Dramatists of the Restoration," *Edinburgh Review*, 72 (1841), 493, 497.
4. H. A. Taine, *History of English Literature*, trans. H. Van Laun (New York: Holt, 1886), I, p. 582.
5. Nicoll, *A History of Restoration Drama, 1660–1700*, pp. 7–8.
6. Joseph Wood Krutch, *Comedy and Conscience after the Restoration* (1924; rev. ed. New York: Columbia Univ. Press, 1949), pp. 24, 44.
7. John Wain, "Restoration Comedy and Its Modern Critics," *EIC*, 6 (1956), 367–68.
8. In *Restoration Drama: Modern Essays in Criticism*, ed. John Loftis (New York: Oxford Univ. Press, 1966), p. 4. Hereafter cited parenthetically.
9. *The Action of English Comedy* (New Haven: Yale Univ. Press, 1970), p. 90. Hereafter cited parenthetically.
10. In *The Development of English Drama in the Late Seventeenth Century*, Robert D. Hume observes that in the modern critical debate about the comedies, "even to those not worried by the idiotic squabble over morality these plays usually seem insufficiently serious or profound" (p. ix). In a word he has demoted the moral issue to the status of an "idiotic squabble," though he devotes many pages to insightful discussion, say, of the kinds of moral responses a late seventeenth-century writer might hope to elicit (p. 39) and to the problems that arise when satiric impact is blurred as a comedy traces the progress of young lovers to a happy resolution (p. 47).

Chapter 2. "The Usefulness of the Stage": Restoration Comedy
Moralisé and the *Réaliste* Tradition

1. "Les Voies de la critique récente: Comment elle étudie la comédie de la restauration," *Etudes Anglaises*, 19 (1966), 413. Norman Holland seems to be the source of Legouis's statistics: "Of six writers, all of whom agree that Restoration comedy was a thoroughly real picture of the life of the court coterie, two find the plays moral, two immoral, and two amoral. Conversely, of four critics who agree that the world of Restoration comedy is 'artificial,' two find the plays immoral and two amoral" (*The First Modern Comedies* [1959; rpt. Bloomington: Indiana Univ. Press, 1967], p. 205). Holland cites his sources—some of which are very minor figures—to show how he arrived at his amusing balance among critics; Legouis does not. Legouis's borrowing is all the more amusing because he disparages Holland's book (pp. 417–18, 420).
2. See Don Cameron Allen, *Mysteriously Meant: The Rediscovery of Pagan Symbolism and Allegorical Interpretation in the Renaissance* (Balti-

Notes to Pages 12–14

more: Johns Hopkins Univ. Press, 1970) for an exhaustive account of how this was done.

3. Holland, *The First Modern Comedies*, p. 8.

4. *The Restoration Comedy of Wit* (Princeton: Princeton Univ. Press, 1952), p. 200.

5. Fujimura offers this passage of purple prose on page 63:

> Finally, fusing all this is the satisfaction one feels in the successful synthesis achieved through the witty apprehension of life. The witty muse dances gaily over the surface of life, thrusting a sharp lance now and then at the torso of mundane existence; its eyes sparkle with gaiety, and there is a radiance in its features at once intellectual and malicious and playful. We are carried away by it, and we join in the dance of the witty muse, content for the moment with its gay whirling. We do not forget the larger issues of life, nor do we flee them, as Lamb suggested; rather we are so affected by the magic touch of the witty muse that we see such issues in a shimmer of beauty, as when the first sun-drenched day of spring sets the dew drops glistening on the flower tips.

Such lyrical outbursts are seldom found in historical criticism of Restoration comedy, I might add.

6. Sigmund Freud, *Civilization and Its Discontents*, trans. James Strachey (New York: Norton, 1962), pp. 89–90.

7. *Life Against Death: The Psychoanalytical Meaning of History* (New York: Random House, 1959), p. 308.

8. The multivalence of such terms as "experience" and "life" as cardinal values in literary criticism will be discussed more extensively later, but it should be noted that after Brown's statement of the problem above, it would be difficult to imagine a pro-death advocate. As Richard King notes in *The Party of Eros: Radical Social Thought and the Realm of Freedom* (Chapel Hill: Univ. of North Carolina Press, 1972), Brown shares with Marcuse, Paul Goodman, and other modern social theorists the desire to combine "instinctual and erotic liberation with political and social radicalism, cultural with political concerns" (p. 50). For a fuller view of the intellectual and ethical matrix of many literary critics, see Philip Rieff, *The Triumph of the Therapeutic* (1966), Theodore Roszak, *The Making of a Counter Culture* (1969), and especially Paul Robinson, *The Freudian Left* (1969).

9. *The Golden Labyrinth: A Study of British Drama* (New York: Norton, 1962), p. 130.

Notes to Pages 15–27

10. "Raillery in Restoration Comedy," *HLQ*, 29 (1966), 159.
11. *Wild Civility: The English Comic Spirit on the Restoration Stage* (Bloomington: Indiana Univ. Press, 1970), p. 136. Hereafter cited parenthetically.
12. "Congreve's Mirabell and the Ideal of the Gentleman," *PMLA*, 79 (1964), 423.
13. *The Comedy of Habit: An Essay on the Use of Courtesy Literature in a Study of Restoration Comic Drama* (Leiden: Universitaire Pers, 1964). In discussing the relation of the audience and the drama, one should proceed cautiously. The articles by Hume and Scouten cited in the Preface, n. 5, are helpful in dispelling some prejudices, and articles on the audience itself are a valuable corrective to the standard literary histories (Beljame, Nicoll, etc.): Emmett L. Avery, "The Restoration Audience," *PQ*, 45 (1966), 54–61, and Harold Love, "The Myth of the Restoration Audience," *Komos*, 1 (1967), 49–56, and "Who were the Restoration Audience?" *Yearbook of English Studies*, 10 (1980), 21–44.
14. "*Préciosite* and the Restoration Comedy of Manners," *HLQ*, 18 (1955), 128.
15. "The Challenge of Restoration Comedy," in *Restoration Drama: Modern Essays in Criticism*, ed. John Loftis (New York: Oxford Univ. Press, 1966), p. 34. Hereafter cited parenthetically.
16. "Marriage of Convenience and the Moral Code of Restoration Comedy," *EIC*, 12 (1962), 376.
17. "L. C. Knights and Restoration Comedy" in *Restoration Drama: Modern Essays in Criticism*, ed. John Loftis (New York: Oxford Univ. Press, 1966), p. 25. Hereafter cited parenthetically.
18. *Amendments of Mr. Collier's False and Imperfect Citations* (London, 1698). Collier's patriotism is doubted on p. 115 because the closing of the theatres, Congreve alleges, would endanger the temperament and thus the political stability of the English people. Congreve makes it nearly a civic obligation to patronize the theatre. See also pp. 84–85, 94–95, and 107. Hereafter cited parenthetically.
19. Dennis, *The Critical Works*, ed. Edward Niles Hooker, 2 vols. (Baltimore: Johns Hopkins Univ. Press, 1939–43), I, 151. Hereafter cited parenthetically.
20. Dennis, *The Critical Works*, II, 245.
21. "Morals of the Restoration," *Sewanee Review*, 24 (1916), 112–13.
22. Vanbrugh, *The Provok'd Wife* (I.i), is the source of Sir John Brute's remarks, while Etherege's *She Wou'd if She Cou'd* (III.iii) provides Sir

Oliver Cockwood's. Such remarks, of course, could be found in numerous other comedies.

23. "Restoration Comedy as Drama of Satire: An Investigation into Seventeenth-Century Aesthetics," *SP*, 61 (1964), 523, 522. Hereafter cited parenthetically.

24. Williams, "Poetical Justice, the Contrivance of Providence, and the Works of William Congreve," *ELH*, 35 (1968), 541. Hereafter cited parenthetically. A much fuller elaboration of this thesis is found in *An Approach to Congreve* (New Haven: Yale Univ. Press, 1979), especially in the first three chapters.

25. *The Ethos of Restoration Comedy* (Urbana: Univ. of Illinois Press, 1971), p. 7. Hereafter cited parenthetically.

Chapter 3. "Escape from this dull age": The *Artificielle* Tradition

1. *The Complete Works of William Hazlitt*, ed. P. P. Howe, 21 vols. (London: Dent, 1930–34), VI, 70.

2. "On the Artificial Comedy of the Last Century" in *Charles Lamb and Elia*, ed. J. E. Morpurgo (Harmondsworth, Middlesex: Penguin, 1948), p. 174. Hereafter cited parenthetically.

3. Walter Houghton's defense of Charles Lamb is almost persuasive, since he contends that Lamb does not mean what he seems to say. If one reads this essay as part of a series on methods of acting, then Lamb appears to be endorsing a particular style of presenting "artificial" comedy. See "Lamb's Criticism of Restoration Comedy," *ELH*, 10 (1943), 61–72.

4. *Dramatic Works* (London, 1840), p. ix. Hereafter cited parenthetically.

5. Hunt's attitude toward "mutilated editions" appears to have changed, for in 1806, while editing *Classic Tales, Serious and Lively*, he excluded *Candide* because of its raciness and "chastened" his texts by using this editorial rationalization: "loose description is seldom missed when it is not found . . . for the generality of readers insensibly become too intent upon what their author is saying, to fancy what he might have said" (Noel Perrin, *Dr. Bowdler's Legacy: A History of Expurgated Books in England and America* [Garden City: Doubleday, 1971], p. 173). If Hunt has bowdlerized the comedies, I have not detected it. The "china scene" in *The Country Wife* is intact, for example, and a quick comparison of other plays with their modern editions indicates that Hunt is faithful to the original text. This editorial courage is not inconsiderable when

one considers his earlier attitude and the tenor of his age, which eagerly purchased "castrated" editions of Shakespeare and "mutilated" Miltons.

6. Critics who rely solely on secondary sources for their historical information are doomed to repeat the errors of those sources. Irène Simon, for example, follows Palmer's book so closely at the beginning of "Restoration Comedy and the Critics," *Revue des Langues Vivantes*, 29 (1963), 397–430, that she repeats several times Palmer's error about the date of Hunt's edition. She does not follow Palmer's dating of Collier's *Short View* as 1697, however. See John Palmer, *The Comedy of Manners* (London: Bell, 1913), p. 275, hereafter cited parenthetically.

7. *Restoration Comedy* (1924; rpt. London: Oxford Univ. Press, 1962), pp. 25–26. Hereafter cited parenthetically.

8. *The Social Mode of Restoration Comedy* (New York: Macmillan, 1926), p. 7. Hereafter cited parenthetically.

9. *Literary Criticism of John Dryden*, ed. Arthur C. Kirsch (Lincoln: Univ. of Nebraska Press, 1966), pp. 97–98.

10. Singh, *The Theory of Drama in the Restoration Period* (Bombay: Orient Longmans, 1963), pp. 71–76. Hereafter cited parenthetically.

Chapter 4. Literature and Moral Persuasion: The Critics' Dilemma

1. Arthur K. Moore, *Contestable Concepts of Literary Theory* (Baton Rouge: Louisiana State Univ. Press, 1973), p. 4.

2. "The Moral Effect of Art," in *The Problems of Aesthetics: A Book of Readings*, ed. Eliseo Vivas and Murray Krieger (New York: Holt, 1953), p. 551.

3. "Sociodicy: A Guide to Modern Usage," *The American Scholar*, 35 (Autumn 1966), 696–714.

4. *The English Epic and Its Background* (London: Chatto and Windus, 1954), p. 12.

5. Emmett L. Avery, "The Restoration Audience," *PQ*, 45 (1966), 54–61; Harold Love, "The Myth of the Restoration Audience," *Komos*, 1 (1967), 49–56, and "Who were the Restoration Audience?" *Yearbook of English Studies*, 10 (1980), 21–44; Arthur H. Scouten and Robert D. Hume, "'Restoration Comedy' and its Audiences, 1660–1776," *Yearbook of English Studies*, 10 (1980), 45–69.

6. Vivas and Krieger, p. 481.

7. *The Report of the Commission on Obscenity and Pornography* (Washington, D.C.: GPO, 1970), p. 26 et passim. The effects of explicit sexual materials are reported on pp. 23–27; the findings on the impact of erot-

Note to Page 54

ica are on pp. 139–263. The chart below (Fig. 1, p. 144), which summarizes presumed harmful and neutral consequences of exposure to erotica, suggests the grounds of the debate about Restoration comedy.

Presumed Consequences of Exposure to Erotica

	Sexual	Nonsexual
Criminal or Generally Regarded as Harmful	1. sexually aggressive acts of a criminal nature 2. unlawful sexual practices 3. nonconsensual sex acts 4. incest 5. sexually perverse behavior 6. adultery 7. illegal sexual activities 8. socially disapproved sexual behavior 9. sexual practices harmful to self 10. deadly serious pursuit of sexual satisfaction 11. dehumanized sexual acts 12. preoccupation (obsession) with sex 13. change direction of sexual development from natural pathway 14. block psychosexual maturation 15. misinformation about sex 16. moral breakdown	17. homicide 18. suicide 19. delinquency 20. criminal acts 21. indecent personal habits 22. unhealthy habits 23. unhealthy thoughts 24. reject reality 25. ennui 26. submission to authoritarianism
Neutral	27. sex attitudes 28. sex values 29. sex information 30. sex habits	

	Presumed Consequences of Exposure to Erotica	
	Sexual	Nonsexual
Beneficial/ Helpful	31. drains off illegitimate sexual desires 32. provides outlet for otherwise frustrated sexual drives 33. releases strong sexual urges without harming others 34. pleasure 35. provides discharge of "antisocial" sexual appetites 36. assists consummation of legitimate sexual responsibilities	

8. "The Stimulating Versus Cathartic Effects of a Vicarious Aggressive Activity," *Journal of Abnormal and Social Psychology*, 63, no. 2 (1961), 381.

9. *Television and Aggression: An Experimental Field Study* (San Francisco: Jossey-Bass, 1971), pp. 140, 141.

10. *Anatomy of Criticism: Four Essays* (Princeton: Princeton Univ. Press, 1957), p. 344.

11. *Selected Essays* (1932; rpt. New York: Harcourt, 1964), p. 347.

12. Quoted in W. K. Wimsatt, Jr., *The Verbal Icon: Studies in the Meaning of Poetry* (1954; rpt. New York: Noonday Press, 1964), p. 87.

13. *Rhetoric*, Bk. II, ch. 1–12.

14. See W. K. Wimsatt, Jr., and Cleanth Brooks, *Literary Criticism: A Short History* (New York: Random House, 1957), p. 36, for an intelligent discussion of the function of catharsis in society, with special attention to the *Poetics, Phaedo*, and the *Politics*.

15. *An Apologie for Poesie*, in *Elizabethan Critical Essays*, ed. G. Gregory Smith, 2 vols. (Oxford: Clarendon Press, 1904), I, 160. Hereafter cited parenthetically.

16. E. D. Hirsch, Jr., "'Intrinsic' Criticism," *College English*, 36 (Dec. 1974), 447.

17. *Literary Criticism of John Dryden*, ed. Arthur C. Kirsch (Lincoln:

Univ. of Nebraska Press, 1966), pp. 97–98. It is not inappropriate to mention that Horace, an authority cited at least as often as Aristotle in contemporary literary disputation, says that poetry can delight or instruct, although the best literature does both. Furthermore, Horace's Dutch commentator, Heinsius, did not attribute to delight the function that Dryden claims he did. I feel that Dryden's views should thus be understood partially in the context of Renaissance aesthetics and partially as the self-serving views of a working dramatist whose livelihood depended on the popular appeal of his work. For a fuller analysis of Dryden's remarks, see Frank Harper Moore, *The Nobler Pleasure: Dryden's Comedy in Theory and Practice* (Chapel Hill: Univ. of North Carolina Press, 1963), pp. 94–96, and John Harrington Smith, *The Gay Couple in Restoration Comedy* (Cambridge: Harvard Univ. Press, 1948), pp. 74–78.

18. *The Yale Edition of the Works of Samuel Johnson*, ed. Arthur Sherbo, 11 vols. (New Haven: Yale Univ. Press, 1958–78), VII, 62. Hereafter cited parenthetically.

19. Jean H. Hagstrum, *Samuel Johnson's Literary Criticism* (1952; rpt. Chicago: Univ. of Chicago Press, 1967), pp. 56–75. This section presents a useful discussion of the relation between ideas of general nature and judicial criticism.

20. *The Mirror and the Lamp: Romantic Theory and Critical Tradition* (1953; rpt. New York: Norton, 1958), pp. 8–20.

21. See Emerson R. Marks, *Relativist and Absolutist: The Early Neoclassical Debate in England* (New Brunswick: Rutgers Univ. Press, 1955). Marks concludes that there are few relativists in the eighteenth century, though some "historical relativists" can be identified. Johnson, for example, could write in *The Lives of the Poets* that "to judge rightly of an author, we must transport ourselves to his time, and examine what were the wants of his contemporaries, and what were his means of supplying them" (Marks, p. 150*n*). But Johnson neither followed this precept in all situations nor accepted the implications of this statement when it came to suspending his ethical judgment, say, of Renaissance or Restoration drama. His strictures on Shakespeare's moral defects insist pointedly that the barbarity of the Elizabethan audience could not excuse his lapses. Thomas A. Hanzo provides a useful study of the conflict between uniformitarian and diversitarian tendencies in Restoration literary criticism, philosophy, theology, and political theory in his *Latitude and Restoration Criticism* (Copenhagen: Rosenkilde and Bagger, 1961). The problem was not resolved during the Restoration, and in the eighteenth century the distinctions hardened into "schools." John-

son remained notably unsympathetic toward innovators in ethics and aesthetics.

22. *The Later Eighteenth Century*, Vol. I of *A History of Modern Criticism, 1750–1950* (New Haven: Yale Univ. Press, 1955), p. 12.

23. *The Great Chain of Being: Essays in the History of an Idea* (1936; rpt. New York: Harper and Row, 1965), p. 294. Hereafter cited parenthetically. For an account of the way in which the "new" epistemology has itself acquired normative powers, see William G. Perry, Jr., *Forms of Intellectual and Ethical Development in the College Years: A Scheme* (New York: Holt, 1970). Perry's remarks on absolutists (p. 131 and pp. 202–3) are the logical extension of tendencies that arose in the eighteenth century and that Arnold was to contend with in the nineteenth century. This interconnection of aesthetics and the "new psychology" is discussed in Ernst Cassirer's study, *The Philosophy of the Enlightenment*, trans. Fritz C. A. Koellner and James P. Pettegrove (Princeton: Princeton Univ. Press, 1951), pp. 298–303. Walter Jackson Bate's *From Classic to Romantic: Premises of Taste in Eighteenth-Century England* (1946; rpt. New York: Harper and Row, 1961) is an especially helpful analysis of the emergence of the romantic sensibility.

24. Matthew Arnold, *The Complete Prose Works of Matthew Arnold*, ed. R. H. Super, 11 vols. (Ann Arbor: Univ. of Michigan Press, 1960–76), V, 123. Subsequent references to Arnold refer to this edition.

25. See "The Literary Influence of Academies," in Vol. III of *The Complete Prose Works*, 232–57.

26. *The Complete Prose Works*, IX, 161.

27. An account of how literature, specifically Dalton Trumbo's *Johnny Got His Gun*, altered the attitude of nursing students toward patients is reported in Janet Nott Holdsworth's study, "Vicarious Experience of Reading a Book in Changing Nursing Students' Attitudes," *Nursing Research*, 17, no. 2 (1968), 135–39. See also n. 7 above.

28. Zink, "The Moral Effect of Art," p. 553.

29. See also Hugh Dalziel Duncan, *Language and Literature in Society* (Chicago: Univ. of Chicago Press, 1953). Graham Hough's account of moral theories of literature is clear and accurate. "A moral theory of literature is without definite content unless it refers to a scheme of moral values existing outside it. It will be the more concrete and explicit the more concrete and explicit this scheme is. . . . More recent theories are often without definite content because they do not refer to any such scheme, only to an inexplicit bundle of prejudices" (*An Essay on Criticism* [New York: Norton, 1966], p. 30).

30. Robert E. Lane, *The Liberties of Wit: Humanism, Criticism, and the Civic Mind* (New Haven: Yale Univ. Press, 1961), pp. 106–7. Hereafter cited parenthetically.

31. *As They Liked It: A Study of Shakespeare's Moral Artistry* (New York: Harper and Row, 1961), p. 57.

32. *Logic and Criticism* (London: Routledge and Kegan Paul, 1963), p. 80.

33. *The Idiom of Poetry*, rev. ed. (Ithaca: Cornell Univ. Press, 1946), pp. 17–18. The key words in Pottle's statement are "right sensibility." For an excellent study of the intellectual background of this concept, see Louis Bredvold's *The Natural History of Sensibility* (Detroit: Wayne State Univ. Press, 1962).

34. *Fiction and the Shape of Belief* (Berkeley: Univ. of California Press, 1964), p. 232. Hereafter cited parenthetically.

35. See p. 232 of *Fiction and the Shape of Belief* for a good summary of these classes of characters.

36. *The Dynamics of Literary Response* (New York: Oxford Univ. Press, 1968), p. xiii. Hereafter cited parenthetically.

37. Holland would be further puzzled to note that Irving Babbitt's "Impressionist Versus Judicial Criticism," *PMLA*, 21 (1906), 687–705, was judged by the members of the Modern Language Association to be one of the three best articles to have appeared in *PMLA* in its first seventy-five years of publication.

38. *Principles of Literary Criticism* (New York: Harcourt, 1925), p. 116.

39. *Art as Experience* (1934; rpt. New York: Putnam's, 1958), pp. 35–57.

40. *Literature and the Sixth Sense* (Boston: Houghton Mifflin, 1969), pp. 21–37.

41. Pp. 50–51.

42. Three books are particularly instructive in this regard: Stanley Edgar Hyman, *The Armed Vision: A Study in the Methods of Modern Literary Criticism* (1948; rpt. New York: Random House, 1955); Murray Krieger, *The New Apologists for Poetry* (Bloomington: Indiana Univ. Press, 1969); and Lee T. Lemon, *The Partial Critics* (New York: Oxford Univ. Press, 1965). Lemon's third chapter deals with edification theories; Krieger studies the intellectual complexities that attend the matter of justifying literature; Hyman studies the aims and achievements of the most important modern critics. But Lemon raises an important theoretical problem later in his study: "By considering the poem as an experience (not loosely or vaguely stimulated by, but at least potentially determined

by, the text), the critic makes the poem a part of the reader's life. Like any other experience, it is suffered and judged. I am arguing that poetry, and art in general, does actually 'test' ideas (and feelings and perceptions) and that once the idea, emotion, or perception is tested it either becomes a part of the total personality of the reader or it does not. If it does not, the test, for whatever reason, has failed" (pp. 170–71). While this appears to be clear and comprehensive, several things are not adequate in this account. First, though we are told that the literary experience is "suffered and judged" as other experiences are, we are not told whether the "judgment" of this experience is to be made by the same criteria that are used to judge those other experiences. Second, the work "passes" the test if it succeeds in becoming part of the reader's total personality. What does this mean, and how can one tell if it has become part of one's "total personality"? If the work becomes part of one's personality, the personality is somehow altered. But is the change necessarily an improvement? In short, the reliance on the experiential touchstone appears to solve more critical problems than are actually solved, for "experience" simply lacks normative powers. The commingling of descriptive and evaluative language in criticism clouds the issue rather than resolves it.

43. Emmett L. Avery, *Congreve's Plays on the Eighteenth-Century Stage* (New York: Modern Language Association, 1951), pp. 14–15.

44. William Righter, *Logic and Criticism* (London: Routledge and Kegan Paul, 1963), p. 53.

45. *Psychoanalysis and Literary Process* (Cambridge, Mass.: Winthrop, 1970), pp. 1–24.

46. "The Fruits of the MLA," found in *The Devils and Canon Barham: Ten Essays on Poets, Novelists, and Monsters* (New York: Farrar, Straus, and Giroux, 1973), pp. 154–202.

47. Righter, *Logic and Criticism*, p. 53.

Chapter 5: "Deep-breathing sex" and Critical Practice

1. Nicoll, *A History of Restoration Drama, 1660–1700*, p. 243.

2. *English Literature of the Late Seventeenth Century* (New York: Oxford Univ. Press, 1969), p. 130.

3. *The Development of English Drama in the Late Seventeenth Century* (Oxford: Clarendon Press, 1976), p. 123.

4. E. D. Hirsch, Jr., considers the belief that good literature necessarily promotes good behavior a rhetorical hat trick ultimately traceable

to Aristotle. "In tacking on the theory of the purgative effect of tragedy, Aristotle performed the first recorded hat trick of intrinsic theory, and in one form or other the trick has been repeated by every good intrinsic critic ever since. I call it a trick not because it is dishonest but because it posits an unwarranted faith in the concordance of quite different kinds of excellence: the excellence of tragedy as tragedy and the excellence of tragedy as therapy. The trick is to assume a harmony of technical and instrumental excellence." See "'Intrinsic' Criticism," *College English*, 36 (Dec. 1974), 446–57.

5. *Likenesses of Truth in Elizabethan and Restoration Drama* (Oxford: Clarendon Press, 1972), p. 25.

6. Morton Bloomfield raises a serious question about modern critics' approach to the meaning of literature. "It is exceedingly fashionable today in the general intellectual flight from history to interpret literature symbolically, or, as it is often called, 'allegorically.' The particularity of fact and event is passed over for the general, the cyclic, and the mythical, which is presumably more universal and more meaningful. Unless the significance of a literary work can be subsumed in a system of metaphor . . . it is assumed to have no real meaning" (p. 73). See "Symbolism in Medieval Literature," *MP*, 56 (Nov. 1958), 73–81.

7. Geoffrey Chaucer, *The Works of Geoffrey Chaucer*, ed. F. N. Robinson, 2nd ed. (Boston: Houghton Mifflin, 1957), 11. 1842–54. For historical criticism of this tale, see Norman T. Harrington, "Chaucer's 'Merchant's Tale': Another Swing of the Pendulum," *PMLA*, 86 (Jan. 1971), 25–31; Paul A. Olson, "Chaucer's Merchant and January's 'Hevene in Erthe Heere,'" *ELH*, 28 (1961), 203–14; Henry Ansgar Kelly, *Love and Marriage in the Age of Chaucer* (Ithaca: Cornell Univ. Press, 1975), pp. 262–332.

8. Montague Summers's *Restoration Comedies* (1922) includes the play but has been long out of print; it is also included in A. Norman Jeffares, *Restoration Comedy*, 4 vols. (London: Folio Press, 1974). For my purposes the first edition (1682) will suffice. Unfortunately, the first edition is very irregularly paginated: for the first twenty-five pages, every page is numbered; thereafter, every other page is numbered. Between pages 35 and 41 two pages are misnumbered and two pages are unnumbered. Act I runs from page 1 to page 13; Act II from page 13 to page 26; Act III from page 26 to page 34; Act IV from 35 to page 41; and Act V runs from page 41 to page 62. All references to the play will be made parenthetically.

9. See Frederick W. Fairholt, ed., *Lord Mayors' Pageants: Being Collec-*

tions Towards a History of these Annual Celebrations (London: Percy Society, 1848).

10. A valuable aspect of Hume's study (*The Development of English Drama in the Late Seventeenth Century*) is his decade-by-decade treatment of theatrical rivalry. See also William Van Lennep et al., *The London Stage, 1660–1800,* 5 pts. in 11 vols. (Carbondale: Southern Illinois Univ. Press, 1960–68).

11. See note 7 above and D. W. Robertson, Jr., *A Preface to Chaucer: Studies in Medieval Perspectives* (Princeton: Princeton Univ. Press, 1962), p. 111 and pp. 375–76.

12. Harrington, "Chaucer's 'Merchant's Tale,'" p. 30.

13. Paul A. Robinson, *The Freudian Left: Wilhelm Reich, Geza Roheim, Herbert Marcuse* (New York: Harper and Row, 1969), pp. 4–5. In *The Party of Eros: Radical Social Thought and the Realm of Freedom* (New York: Dell, 1973), Richard King argues that such social theorists as Brown and Marcuse tend "to make public all private aspects of existence; to metaphorically see the bedroom as the battleground for change; in short, as Reich put it, to politicize sex" (p. 8).

14. Sarup Singh, *The Theory of Drama in the Restoration Period* (Bombay: Orient Longmans, 1963). See also Hume, *The Development of English Drama in the Late Seventeenth Century,* pp. 32–62. That contemporary theory differed from practice is important to note. The dramatists' pious ejaculations about the moral usefulness of their comedies should not be read without some sense of irony.

15. Jack Gould, "Can Bigotry Be Laughed Away? It's Worth a Try," *New York Times* (21 February 1971), Sec. 2, p. 15.

16. Ibid., p. 12.

17. Laura Hobson, "As I listened to Archie Say 'Hebe' . . ." *New York Times* (12 September 1971), sec. 2, p. 12.

18. "Some Problems in the Theory of Comedy," *Journal of Aesthetics and Art Criticism,* 31 (1972), 99. Hereafter cited parenthetically.

19. *The Country Wife,* ed. Thomas H. Fujimura (Lincoln: Univ. of Nebraska Press, 1965), p. 6. All citations are to this text and will be placed parenthetically.

20. See Anthony Kaufman, "Wycherley's *The Country Wife* and the Don Juan Character," *ECS,* 9 (Winter 1975–76), 216–31. Kaufman's essay does not provide a very adequate account of the Harcourt-Alithea subplot and assumes that the audience will respond to Horner as he does, regardless of the actor's interpretation of the role.

Notes to Pages 111–122

21. In *Validity in Interpretation* (New Haven: Yale Univ. Press, 1967), E. D. Hirsch, Jr., observes that much modern criticism implicitly denies "the possibility of validity in any absolute or normative sense of the word. The wider implications of such hermeneutical skepticism are usually overlooked by its adherents. At stake ultimately is the right of any humanistic discipline to claim genuine knowledge. Since all humane studies . . . are founded upon the interpretation of texts, valid interpretation is crucial to the validity of all subsequent inferences in those studies. The theoretical aim of a genuine discipline, scientific or humanistic, is the attainment of truth, and its practical aim is agreement that truth has probably been achieved" (pp. viii–ix).

22. George L. Scheper, "Reformation Attitudes toward Allegory and the Song of Songs," *PMLA*, 89 (1974), 558.

Chapter 6. "Duels, Claps, and Bastards": The Problem of Sympathy and Judgment

1. Robert D. Hume, *The Development of English Drama in the Late Seventeenth Century* (Oxford: Clarendon Press, 1976), p. 97.

2. See Robert D. Hume, "Otway and the Comic Muse," *SP*, 73 (Jan. 1976), 87–116 and Jean H. Hagstrum, *Sex and Sensibility: Ideal and Erotic Love from Milton to Mozart* (Chicago: Univ. of Chicago Press, 1980), pp. 90–100.

3. Robert D. Hume, "Marital Discord in English Comedy from Dryden to Fielding," *MP*, 74 (Feb. 1977), 248–72.

4. *The Works of Thomas Otway*, ed. J. C. Ghosh, 2 vols., (Oxford: Clarendon Press, 1932), II, pp. 102–3. All references to Otway's comedies are from this volume; pages are cited in the text.

5. At critical moments in his fantasies, Sir Jolly interrupts himself—or is interrupted by others. See pp. 107, 112–13, 139, and 191.

6. The OED records no instance of "mowze," though its meaning is clear from its rhymed synonyms.

7. I find the thesis of Aubrey Williams inapplicable to this and many others comedies of the period. For a recent statement of his views, see "Of 'One Faith': Authors and Auditors in the Restoration Theatre," *Studies in the Literary Imagination*, 10 (Spring 1977), 57–76.

8. P. 122. Otway uses the same kinds of tableaus in *The Atheist*, deriding childhood (p. 299) and military service (p. 300) and celebrating freedom (p. 328).

9. Simply put, the ethos of Otway's comedies is similar to that of

his tragedies. The perfidy of human relationships is central: soldiers are betrayed by their country and children by their parents; not even partners-in-crime are trustworthy (e.g., Sir Jolly and Sir Davy); the soldiers' fortune is poverty; the atheist seeks a priest when frightened, but the priest is a fraud intent on learning the names of the atheist's mistresses. Ethical issues raised in the comedies are also found in *The Orphan* (1680) and *Venice Preserved* (1682). In *The Orphan* is a bitter picture of corruption in court life, and the deception of one brother by another is especially painful; in *Venice Preserved* the plot includes the conspiracy of a son-in-law against father-in-law, which compromises the loyalty of a woman who must choose between husband and father. Otway's persistent concern with ethical choices in a very fallen world suggests a seriousness that most critics have not recognized.

10. The watch announces the time as 4:00 A.M. in Act V (p. 187).

11. See Robert D. Hume, "The Myth of the Rake in 'Restoration' Comedy," *Studies in the Literary Imagination*, 10 (Spring 1977), 25–55.

12. *Complete Works*, ed. Montague Summers, 5 vols. (London: Fortune Press, 1927), IV, 204. All references to *The Squire of Alsatia* are from volume 4 of this edition; pages are cited in the text.

13. *A History of Restoration Drama, 1660–1700*, p. 198.

14. "'Restoration Comedy' and Its Audiences, 1660–1776," *Yearbook of English Studies*, 10 (1980), 56.

15. The theme of the prodigal father, a feature both of *The Atheist* and *The Squire of Alsatia*, suggests that for Otway and Shadwell no father will provide a completely adequate model.

16. See also Robert D. Hume, "Formal Intention in *The Brothers* and *The Squire of Alsatia*," *ELN*, 6 (1969), 176–84, and Hume, *The Development of English Drama in the Late Seventeenth Century*, pp. 78–86.

17. See also pp. 238, 240, 248, 274, and 276.

18. "Myth of the Rake in 'Restoration' Comedy," p. 36.

19. On p. 219 and p. 221, Sir Edward and Sir William, using nearly the same language, accuse each other of unwillingness or inability to see their sons as they are. Their sons' vision is not much better.

20. Shirley Strum Kenny, "Humane Comedy," *MP*, 75 (Aug. 1977), 29–43.

21. Richard Levin, *New Readings vs. Old Plays: Recent Trends in the Reinterpretation of English Renaissance Drama* (Chicago: University of Chicago Press, 1979), pp. 78–145.

22. Especially notable contributions include Hume, *The Development of English Drama in the Late Seventeenth Century*; the California Dryden and

other new editions of major and minor dramatists by other university presses; *The London Stage*; and the encyclopedic *Biographical Dictionary* by Philip Highfill, Jr., Kalman Burnim, and Edward Langhans.

23. See chap. 4, n. 5.

24. See John Wallace, "Dryden and History: A Problem in Allegorical Reading," *ELH*, 36 (Mar. 1969), 265–90, and "'Examples are Best Precepts': Readers and Meanings in Seventeenth-Century Poetry," *Critical Inquiry*, 1 (Dec. 1974), 273–90.

25. Hume, *The Development of English Drama in the Late Seventeenth Century*, pp. 32–62.

26. For vigorous attempts to explain how literature "works," see Norman N. Holland, *The Dynamics of Literary Response* (New York: Oxford Univ. Press, 1968) and *5 Readers Reading* (New Haven: Yale Univ. Press, 1975); Louise Rosenblatt, *The Reader, The Text, The Poem* (Carbondale: Southern Illinois Univ. Press, 1978) and her pioneering study, *Literature as Exploration*, rev. ed. (New York: Noble and Noble, 1968); Alan C. Purves and Richard Beach, *Literature and the Reader* (Urbana, Ill.: NCTE, 1972); and Stanley Fish, *Surprised by Sin: The Reader in Paradise Lost* (London: Macmillan, 1967), *Self-Consuming Artifacts: The Experience of Seventeenth-Century Literature* (Berkeley: Univ. of California Press, 1972), and *Is There a Text in the Class?* (Cambridge: Harvard Univ. Press, 1980); for a useful review of current research, see David Bleich, "The Identity of Pedagogy and Research in the Study of Response to Literature," *College English*, 42 (Dec. 1980), 350–66.

Selected Bibliography

ARTICLES

AVERY, EMMETT, L. "The Restoration Audience." *PQ,* 45 (1966), 54–61.

BABBITT, IRVING. "Impressionist *Versus* Judicial Criticism." *PMLA,* 21 (1906), 687–705.

BATESON, F. W. "L. C. Knights and Restoration Comedy." In *Restoration Drama: Modern Essays in Criticism.* Ed. John Loftis. New York: Oxford Univ. Press, 1966.

———. "Second Thoughts: II. L. C. Knights and Restoration Comedy." *Essays in Criticism,* 7 (1957), 56–67.

BELL, DANIEL. "Sociodicy: A Guide to Modern Usage." *The American Scholar,* 35 (Autumn 1966), 696–714.

BERKELEY, DAVID S. "*Préciosité* and the Restoration Comedy of Manners." *HLQ,* 18 (1955), 109–28.

BERKOWITZ, LEONARD, and EDNA RAWLINGS. "Effects of Film Violence on Inhibitions Against Subsequent Aggression." *Journal of Abnormal and Social Psychology,* 66, No. 5 (1963), 405–12.

BLEICH, DAVID. "The Identity of Pedagogy and Research in the Study of Response to Literature." *College English,* 42 (Dec. 1980), 350–66.

BLOOMFIELD, MORTON. "Symbolism in Medieval Literature." *MP,* 56 (Nov. 1958), 73–81.

CECIL, C. D. "Delicate and Indelicate Puns in Restoration Comedy." *MLR,* 61 (1966), 572–78.

———. "Libertine and Précieux Elements in Restoration Comedy." *Essays in Criticism,* 9 (1959), 239–53.

———. "Raillery in Restoration Comedy." *HLQ,* 29 (1966), 147–59.

CRAWFORD, BARTHOLOW V. "High Comedy in Terms of Restoration Practice." *PQ,* 8 (1929), 339–47.

DRAPER, JOHN W. "The Theory of the Comic in Eighteenth-Century England." *JEGP,* 37 (1938), 207–23.

Selected Bibliography

EMPSON, WILLIAM. "Restoration Comedy Again." *Essays in Criticism*, 7 (1957), 318.

FESHBACH, SEYMOUR. "The Stimulating Versus Cathartic Effects of a Vicarious Aggressive Activity." *Journal of Abnormal and Social Psychology*, 63, No. 2 (1961), 381–85.

GAGEN, JEAN. "Congreve's Mirabell and the Ideal of the Gentleman." *PMLA*, 79 (1964), 422–27.

GOULD, JACK. "Can Bigotry Be Laughed Away? It's Worth a Try." *New York Times*, 21 February 1971, Sec. 2, p. 15.

HARRINGTON, NORMAN T. "Chaucer's 'Merchant's Tale': Another Swing of the Pendulum." *PMLA*, 86 (Jan. 1971), 25–31.

HIRSCH, E. D., JR. "'Intrinsic' Criticism." *College English*, 36 (Dec. 1974), 446–57.

HOBSON, LAURA. "As I Listened to Archie Say 'Hebe' . . ." *New York Times*, 12 September 1971, Sec. 2, p. 1.

HOLDSWORTH, JANET NOTT. "Vicarious Experience of Reading a Book in Changing Nursing Students' Attitudes." *Nursing Research*, 17, No. 2 (1968), 135–39.

HOUGHTON, WALTER E., JR. "Lamb's Criticism of Restoration Comedy." *ELH*, 10 (1943), 61–72.

HUGHES, LEO. "Attitudes of Some Restoration Dramatists toward Farce." *PQ*, 19 (1940), 268–87.

HUME, ROBERT D. "Diversity and Development in Restoration Comedy, 1660–1679." *Eighteenth-Century Studies*, 5 (Spring 1972), 365–97.

———. "Formal Intention in *The Brothers* and *The Squire of Alsatia*." *ELN*, 6 (Mar. 1969), 176–84.

———. "Marital Discord in English Comedy from Dryden to Fielding." *MP*, 74 (Feb. 1977), 248–72.

———. "The Myth of the Rake in 'Restoration' Comedy." *Studies in the Literary Imagination*, 10 (Spring 1977), 25–55.

———. "Otway and the Comic Muse." *SP*, 73 (Jan. 1976), 87–116.

———. "Some Problems in the Theory of Comedy." *Journal of Aesthetics and Art Criticism*, 31 (1972), 87–100.

KAUFMAN, ANDREW. "Wycherley's *The Country Wife* and the Don Juan Character." *ECS*, 9 (Winter 1975–76), 216–31.

KENNY, SHIRLEY STRUM. "Humane Comedy." *MP*, 75 (Aug. 1977), 29–43.

KNIGHTS, L. C. "Restoration Comedy: The Reality and the Myth." In *Restoration Drama: Modern Essays in Criticism*. Ed. John Loftis. New York: Oxford Univ. Press, 1966.

LAMB, CHARLES. "On the Artificial Comedy of the Lost Century." In

Selected Bibliography

Charles Lamb and Elia. Ed. J. E. Morpurgo. Harmondsworth, Middlesex: Penguin, 1948.

LEGOUIS, PIERRE. "Les Voies de la critique récente: Comment elle étudie la comédie de la restauration." *Etudes Anglaises,* 19 (1966), 412–23.

LOFTIS, JOHN. "The Limits of Historical Veracity in Neoclassical Drama." In *England in the Restoration and Early Eighteenth Century: Essays on Culture and Society.* Ed. H. T. Swedenberg, Jr. Berkeley: Univ. of California Press, 1972.

———. "The Social Milieu of Early Eighteenth-Century Comedy." *MP,* 53 (1955), 100–112.

LOVE, HAROLD. "The Myth of the Restoration Audience." *Komos,* 1 (1967), 49–56.

———. "Who were the Restoration Audience?" *Yearbook of English Studies,* 10 (1980), 21–44.

MACAULAY, THOMAS BABINGTON. "Comic Dramatists of the Restoration." *Edinburgh Review,* 72 (1841), 490–528.

MCDONALD, CHARLES O. "Restoration Comedy as Drama of Satire: An Investigation into Seventeenth-Century Aesthetics." *SP,* 61 (1964), 522–44.

MCGALLIARD, JOHN C. "Chaucerian Comedy: 'The Merchant's Tale,' Jonson, and Molière." *PQ,* 25 (1946), 343–70.

MEREDITH, GEORGE. "An Essay on Comedy." In *Comedy.* Ed. Wylie Sypher. Garden City, N.Y.: Doubleday, 1956.

MILES, DUDLEY. "Morals of the Restoration." *Sewanee Review,* 24 (1916), 105–14.

MILLER, HENRY KNIGHT. "The 'Whig Interpretation' of Literary History." *ECS,* 6 (1972), 60–84.

MONTGOMERY, GUY. "The Challenge of Restoration Comedy." In *Restoration Drama: Modern Essays in Criticism.* Ed. John Loftis. New York: Oxford Univ. Press, 1966.

OLSON, PAUL A. "Chaucer's Merchant and January's 'Hevene in Erthe Heere.'" *ELH,* 28 (1961), 203–14.

SCHEPER, GEORGE L. "Reformation Attitudes toward Allegory and the Song of Songs." *PMLA,* 89 (1974), 551–62.

SCOUTEN, ARTHUR H. "Notes Toward a History of Restoration Comedy." *PQ,* 45 (1966), 62–70.

SCOUTEN, ARTHUR H., and ROBERT D. HUME, "'Restoration Comedy' and its Audiences, 1660–1776," *Yearbook of English Studies,* 10 (1980), 45–69.

SIMON, IRÈNE. "Restoration Comedy and the Critics." *Revue des Langues*

Selected Bibliography

Vivantes, 29 (1963), 397–430.
STOLL, ELMER E. "'Artificial Comedy.'" *TLS,* 1 March 1928, p. 150.
———. "The *Beau Monde* at the Restoration." *MLN,* 49 (1934), 425–32.
———. "Literature No 'Document.'" *MLR,* 19 (1924), 141–57.
———. "'Real Society' in Restoration Comedy: Hymeneal Pretenses." *MLN,* 58 (1943), 175–81.
TRAUGOTT, JOHN. "The Rake's Progress from Court to Comedy: A Study in Comic Form." *SEL,* 6 (1966), 381–407.
VERNON, P. F. "Marriage of Convenience and the Moral Code of Restoration Comedy." *EIC,* 12 (1962), 370–87.
WAIN, JOHN. "Restoration Comedy and Its Modern Critics." *EIC,* 6 (1956), 367–85.
WALLACE, JOHN. "Dryden and History: A Problem in Allegorical Reading." *ELH,* 36 (Mar. 1969), 265–90.
———. "'Examples are Best Precepts': Readers and Meanings in Seventeenth-Century Poetry." *Critical Inquiry,* 1 (Dec. 1974), 273–90.
WILLIAMS, AUBREY. "Of 'One Faith': Authors and Auditors in the Restoration Theatre." *Studies in the Literary Imagination,* 10 (Spring 1977), 57–76.
———. "Poetical Justice, the Contrivances of Providence, and the Works of William Congreve." *ELH,* 35 (1968), 540–65.
ZINK, SIDNEY. "The Moral Effect of Art." In *The Problems of Aesthetics: A Book of Readings.* Ed. Eliseo Vivas and Murry Krieger. New York: Holt, 1953.

BOOKS

ABRAMS, M. H. *The Mirror and the Lamp: Romantic Theory and the Critical Tradition.* 1953; rpt. New York: Norton, 1958.
ALLEN, D. C. *Mysteriously Meant: The Rediscovery of Pagan Symbolism and Allegorical Interpretation in the Renaissance.* Baltimore: Johns Hopkins Univ. Press, 1970.
ANTHONY, SR. ROSE. *The Jeremy Collier Stage Controversy: 1698–1726.* Milwaukee: Marquette Univ. Press, 1937.
ARISTOTLE. *The Poetics.* Trans. S. H. Butcher. 4th ed. London: Macmillan, 1907.
ARNOLD, MATTHEW. *The Complete Prose Works of Matthew Arnold.* Ed. R. H. Super. 11 vols. Ann Arbor: Univ. of Michigan Press, 1960–76.
AVERY, EMMETT L. *Congreve's Plays on the Eighteenth-Century Stage.* New York: Modern Language Association, 1951.

Selected Bibliography

AVERY, EMMETT L., AND ARTHUR H. SCOUTEN. *The London Stage, 1660–1700: A Critical Introduction.* Carbondale: Southern Illinois Univ. Press, 1968.
BATE, WALTER JACKSON. *From Classic to Romantic: Premises of Taste in Eighteenth-Century England.* 1946; rpt. New York: Harper and Row, 1961.
BATESON, F. W. *English Comic Drama, 1700–1750.* Oxford: The Clarendon Press, 1929.
BELJAME, ALEXANDRE. *Men of Letters and the English Public in the Eighteenth Century, 1660–1744: Dryden, Addison and Pope.* Trans. E. O. Lorimer. Ed. Bonamy Dobrée. London: Kegan Paul, Trench, Trubner, 1948.
BIRDSALL, VIRGINIA OGDEN. *Wild Civility: The English Comic Spirit on the Restoration Stage.* Bloomington: Indiana Univ. Press, 1970.
BREDVOLD, LOUIS. *The Natural History of Sensibility.* Detroit: Wayne State Univ. Press, 1962.
BROWN, JOHN RUSSELL, and BERNARD HARRIS, eds. *Restoration Theatre.* New York: St. Martin's Press, 1967.
BROWN, NORMAN O. *Life Against Death: The Psychoanalytic Meaning of History.* New York: Random House, 1959.
CASSIRER, ERNST. *The Philosophy of the Enlightenment.* Trans. Fritz C. A. Koellner and James P. Pettegrove. Princeton: Princeton Univ. Press, 1951.
CHAUCER, GEOFFREY. *The Works of Geoffrey Chaucer.* Ed. F. N. Robinson, 2nd ed. Boston: Houghton Mifflin, 1957.
COLLIER, JEREMY. *A Defense of the Short View.* London, 1699.
———. *A Short View of the Immorality and Profaneness of the English Stage.* London, 1698.
CONGREVE, WILLIAM. *Amendments of Mr. Collier's False and Imperfect Citations.* London, 1698.
CREWS, FREDERICK, ed. *Psychoanalysis and Literary Process.* Cambridge, Mass: Winthrop, 1970.
DENNIS, JOHN. *The Critical Works of John Dennis.* 2 vols. Ed. Edward Niles Hooker. Baltimore: The Johns Hopkins Univ. Press, 1939–43.
DEWEY, JOHN. *Art as Experience.* 1934; rpt., New York: Putnam's, 1958.
DOBRÉE, BONAMY. *Restoration Comedy, 1660–1720.* 1924; rpt. London: Oxford Univ. Press, 1962.
DRYDEN, JOHN. *Literary Criticism of John Dryden.* Ed. Arthur C. Kirsch. Lincoln: Univ. of Nebraska Press, 1966.

Selected Bibliography

DUNCAN, HUGH DALZIEL. *Language and Literature in Society: A Sociological Essay on Theory and Method in the Interpretation of Linguistic Symbols. With a Bibliographical Guide to the Sociology of Literature.* Chicago: Univ. of Chicago Press, 1953.
ELIOT, T. S. *Selected Essays.* 1932; rpt. New York: Harcourt, 1964.
ETHEREGE, GEORGE. *The Man of Mode.* Ed. W. B. Carnochan. Lincoln: Univ. of Nebraska Press, 1966.
FAIRHOLT, FREDERICK W., ed. *Lord Mayors' Pageants: Being Collections Towards a History of these Annual Celebrations.* London: Percy Society, 1848.
FESHBACH, SEYMOUR, and ROBERT D. SINGER. *Television and Aggression: An Experimental Field Study.* San Francisco: Jossey-Bass, 1971.
FISH, STANLEY. *Is There a Text in the Class?* Cambridge: Harvard Univ. Press, 1980.
———. *Self-Consuming Artifacts: The Experience of Seventeenth-Century Literature.* Berkeley: Univ. of California Press, 1972.
———. *Surprised by Sin: The Reader in Paradise Lost.* London: Macmillan, 1967.
FREUD, SIGMUND. *Civilization and Its Discontents.* Trans. James Strachey. New York: Norton, 1962.
———. *Wit and Its Relation to the Unconscious.* Authorized English ed. With Introduction by A. A. Brill. New York: Moffat, Yard, 1916.
FRYE, NORTHROP. *Anatomy of Criticism: Four Essays.* Princeton: Princeton Univ. Press, 1957.
———. *The Well-Tempered Critic.* Bloomington: Indiana Univ. Press, 1963.
FUJIMURA, THOMAS H. *The Restoration Comedy of Wit.* Princeton: Princeton Univ. Press, 1952.
GARDNER, JOHN. *On Moral Fiction.* New York: Basic Books, 1978.
HAGSTRUM, JEAN H. *Samuel Johnson's Literary Criticism.* 1952; rpt. Chicago: Univ. of Chicago Press, 1967.
———. *Sex and Sensibility: Ideal and Erotic Love from Milton to Mozart.* Chicago: Univ. of Chicago Press, 1980.
HAMILTON, ANTHONY. *The Memoirs of the Count de Grammont.* Trans. Peter Quennell. With introduction by Cyril Hughes Hartmann. 1890; rpt. New York: E. P. Dutton, 1930.
HANZO, THOMAS A. *Latitude and Restoration Criticism.* Copenhagen: Rosenkilde and Bagger, 1961.
HARBAGE, ALFRED. *As They Liked It: A Study of Shakespeare's Moral Artistry.* New York: Harper and Row, 1961.

Selected Bibliography

HAWKINS, HARRIET. *Likenesses of Truth in Elizabethan and Restoration Drama.* Oxford: Clarendon Press, 1972.

HAZLITT, WILLIAM. *The Complete Works of William Hazlitt.* Ed. P. P. Howe. 21 vols. London: Dent, 1930–34.

HIGHFILL, PHILIP H., JR., KALMAN A. BURNIM, and EDWARD A. LANGHANS. *A Biographical Dictionary of Actors, Actresses, Musicians, Dancers, Managers and Other Stage Personnel in London, 1660–1800.* 16 vols. in progress. 6 vols. to date. Carbondale: Southern Illinois Univ. Press, 1973–.

HIRSCH, E. D., JR. *Validity in Interpretation.* New Haven: Yale Univ. Press, 1967.

HOLLAND, NORMAN N. *The Dynamics of Literary Response.* New York: Oxford University Press, 1968.

————. *The First Modern Comedies: The Significance of Etherege, Wycherley, and Congreve.* 1959; rpt. Bloomington: Indiana Univ. Press, 1967.

————. *5 Readers Reading.* New Haven: Yale Univ. Press, 1975.

HOUGH, GRAHAM. *An Essay on Criticism.* New York: Norton, 1966.

HUIZINGA, JOHN. *Homo Ludens: A Study of the Play Element in Culture.* 1949; rpt. London: Maurice Temple Smith, 1970.

HUME, ROBERT D. *The Development of English Drama in the Late Seventeenth Century.* Oxford: Clarendon Press, 1976.

HUNT, LEIGH, ed. *The Dramatic Works of Wycherley, Congreve, Vanbrugh, and Farquhar With Biographical and Critical Notices.* London, 1840.

HYMAN, STANLEY EDGAR. *The Armed Vision: A Study in the Methods of Modern Literary Criticism.* 1948; rpt. New York: Random House, 1955.

JEFFARES, A. NORMAN, ed. *Restoration Comedy.* 4 vols. London: Folio Press, 1974.

JOHNSON, SAMUEL. *Johnson on Shakespeare.* Ed. Arthur Sherbo. 3 vols. New Haven: Yale Univ. Press, 1968.

————. *Lives of the Poets.* Ed. George Birkbeck Hill. 3 vols. 1905; rpt. New York: Octagon Books, 1967.

————. *The Yale Edition of the Works of Samuel Johnson.* Ed. Arthur Sherbo. 11 vols. New Haven: Yale Univ. Press, 1958–78.

KAUL, ARNOLD. *The Action of English Comedy.* New Haven: Yale Univ. Press, 1970.

KELLY, HENRY ANSGAR. *Love and Marriage in the Age of Chaucer.* Ithaca: Cornell Univ. Press, 1975.

KING, RICHARD. *The Party of Eros: Radical Social Thought and the Realm of Freedom.* New York: Dell, 1973.

KNIGHT, G. WILSON. *The Golden Labyrinth: A Study of British Drama.* New

Selected Bibliography

York: Norton, 1962.
KRIEGER, MURRAY. *The New Apologists for Poetry.* Bloomington: Indiana Univ. Press, 1969.
KROOK, DOROTHEA. *Three Traditions of Moral Thought.* Cambridge: Cambridge University Press, 1959.
KRUTCH, JOSEPH WOOD. *Comedy and Conscience after the Restoration.* 1924; rev. ed. New York: Columbia Univ. Press, 1949.
LANE, ROBERT E. *The Liberties of Wit: Humanism, Criticism, and the Civic Mind.* New Haven: Yale Univ. Press, 1961.
LASLETT, PETER. *The World We Have Lost.* New York: Scribner's, 1966.
LEAVIS, F. R. *The Common Pursuit.* London: Chatto and Windus, 1952.
———. *The Great Tradition: George Eliot, Henry James, Joseph Conrad.* New York: New York Univ. Press, 1969.
LEMON, LEE T. *The Partial Critics.* New York: Oxford Univ. Press, 1965.
LEVIN, RICHARD. *New Readings vs. Old Plays: Recent Trends in the Reinterpretation of English Renaissance Drama.* Chicago: Univ. of Chicago Press, 1979.
LEWIS, C. S. *A Preface to Paradise Lost.* 1942; rpt. New York: Oxford Univ. Press, 1961.
LOFTIS, JOHN, ED. *Restoration Drama: Modern Essays in Criticism.* New York: Oxford Univ. Press, 1966.
LOVEJOY, A. O. *The Great Chain of Being: Essays in the History of An Idea.* 1936; rpt. New York: Harper and Row, 1965.
LOWENTHAL, LEO. *Literature, Popular Culture, and Society.* Englewood Cliffs, N. J.: Prentice-Hall, 1961.
LYNCH, KATHLEEN. *The Social Mode of Restoration Comedy.* New York: Macmillan, 1926.
MARKS, EMERSON R. *Relativist and Absolutist: The Early Neoclassical Debate in England.* New Brunswick: Rutgers Univ. Press, 1955.
MINER, EARL, ed. *Restoration Dramatists: A Collection of Critical Essays.* Englewood Cliffs, N.J.: Prentice-Hall, 1966.
MOORE, ARTHUR K. *Contestable Concepts of Literary Theory.* Baton Rouge: Louisiana State Univ. Press, 1973.
MOORE, FRANK HARPER. *The Nobler Pleasure: Dryden's Comedy in Theory and Practice.* Chapel Hill: Univ. of North Carolina Press, 1963.
NICOLL, ALLARDYCE. *A History of Restoration Drama, 1660–1700.* 4th ed. Vol. I of *A History of English Drama, 1660–1900.* Cambridge: Cambridge Univ. Press, 1952.
OTWAY, THOMAS. *The Works of Thomas Otway.* Ed. J. C. Ghosh. 2 vols. Oxford: Clarendon Press, 1932.

Selected Bibliography

PALMER, JOHN. *The Comedy of Manners.* London: Bell, 1913.
PEACOCK, R. *Criticism and Personal Taste.* Oxford: Clarendon Press, 1972.
PEPYS, SAMUEL. *The Diary of Samuel Pepys.* 11 vols. in progress. Ed. Robert Latham and William Matthews. Berkeley: Univ. of California Press, 1970–.
PERRIN, NOEL. *Dr. Bowdler's Legacy: A History of Expurgated Books in England and America.* New York: Doubleday, 1971.
PERRY, WILLIAM G. *Forms of Intellectual and Ethical Development in the College Years: A Scheme.* New York: Holt, 1970.
POTTLE, FREDERICK A. *The Idiom of Poetry.* Rev. ed. Ithaca: Cornell Univ. Press, 1946.
PURVES, ALAN C., and RICHARD BEACH. *Literature and the Reader: Research in Response to Literature, Reading Interests, and the Teaching of Literature.* Urbana, Ill. NCTE, 1972.
RAHV, PHILIP. *Literature and the Sixth Sense.* Boston: Houghton Mifflin, 1969.
RAVENSCROFT, EDWARD. *The London Cuckolds.* London, 1682.
The Report of the Commission on Obscenity and Pornography. Washington, D.C.: GPO, 1970.
RICHARDS, I. A. *Principles of Literary Criticism.* New York: Harcourt, 1925.
RIEFF, PHILLIP. *The Triumph of the Therapeutic: Uses of Faith after Freud.* New York: Harper and Row, 1966.
RIGHTER, WILLIAM. *Logic and Criticism.* London: Routledge and Kegan Paul, 1963.
ROBERTSON, D. W., JR. *A Preface to Chaucer: Studies in Medieval Perspectives.* Princeton: Princeton Univ. Press, 1962.
ROBINSON, PAUL A. *The Freudian Left: Wilhelm Reich, Geza Roheim, Herbert Marcuse.* New York: Harper and Row, 1969.
ROSENBLATT, LOUISE. *Literature as Exploration.* Rev. ed. New York: Noble and Noble, 1968.
———. *The Reader, the Text, the Poem: The Transactional Theory of the Literary Work.* Carbondale: Southern Illinois Univ. Press, 1978.
ROSZAK, THEODORE. *The Making of a Counter Culture: Reflections on the Technocratic Society and Its Youthful Opposition.* Garden City, N.Y.: Doubleday, 1969.
RYMER, THOMAS. *The Critical Works of Thomas Rymer.* Ed. Curt A. Zimansky. New Haven: Yale Univ. Press, 1956.
SACKS, SHELDON. *Fiction and the Shape of Belief: A Study of Henry Fielding,*

Selected Bibliography

with *Glances at Swift, Johnson, and Richardson.* Berkeley: Univ. of California Press, 1964.
SANTAYANA, GEORGE. *The Life of Reason; or, The Phases of Human Progress.* 5 vols. New York: Scribner's 1905–26.
SCHNEIDER, BEN ROSS. *The Ethos of Restoration Comedy.* Urbana: Univ. of Illinois Press, 1971.
SHADWELL, THOMAS. *The Complete Works of Thomas Shadwell.* Ed. Montague Summers. 5 vols. London: Fortune Press, 1927.
SHARMA, ROM CHANDRA. *Themes and Conventions in the Comedy of Manners.* New York: Asia Publishing House, 1965.
SIDNEY, SIR PHILIP. *An Apologie for Poetry.* In *Elizabethan Critical Essays.* Ed. G. Gregory Smith. 2 vols. Oxford: Clarendon Press, 1904.
SINGH, SARUP. *The Theory of Drama in the Restoration Period.* Bombay: Orient Longmans, 1963.
SMITH, JOHN HARRINGTON. *The Gay Couple in Restoration Comedy.* Cambridge: Harvard Univ. Press, 1948.
SUMMERS, MONTAGUE, ed. *Restoration Comedies: "The Parsons Wedding," "The London Cuckolds," and "Sir Courtly Nice, or, It Cannot Be."* Boston: Small, Maynard, 1922.
SUTHERLAND, JAMES. *English Literature of the Late Seventeenth Century.* New York: Oxford Univ. Press, 1969.
TAINE, H. A. *History of English Literature.* 2 vols. Trans. H. Van Laun. 1883; rpt. New York: Ungar, 1965.
TILLYARD, E. M. W. *The English Epic and Its Background.* London: Chatto and Windus, 1954.
UNDERWOOD, DALE. *Etherege and the Seventeenth-Century Comedy of Manners.* New Haven: Yale Univ. Press, 1957.
VAN LENNEP, WILLIAM, EMMETT L. AVERY, ARTHUR H. SCOUTEN, GEORGE WINCHESTER STONE, JR., and CHARLES BEECHER HOGAN. *The London Stage, 1660–1800.* 5 pts. in 11 vols. Carbondale: Southern Illinois Univ. Press, 1960–68.
WELLEK, RENÉ. *The Later Eighteenth Century.* Vol. I of *A History of Modern Criticism, 1750–1950.* New Haven: Yale Univ. Press, 1955.
WELLEK, RENÉ, and AUSTIN WARREN. *Theory of Literature.* 3rd ed. New York: Harcourt, 1956.
WILKINSON, D. R. M. *The Comedy of Habit: An Essay on the Use of Courtesy Literature in a Study of Restoration Comic Drama.* Leiden: Unversitaire Pers, 1964.
WILLIAMS, AUBREY L. *An Approach to Congreve.* New Haven: Yale Univ. Press, 1979.

Selected Bibliography

WILSON, EDMUND. *The Devils and Canon Barhan: Ten Essays on Poets, Novelists, and Monsters.* New York: Farrar, Straus, and Giroux, 1973.

WIMSATT, W. K., JR. *The Verbal Icon: Studies in the Meaning of Poetry.* 1954; rpt. New York: Noonday Press, 1964.

WIMSATT, W. K., JR., and CLEANTH BROOKS. *Literary Criticism: A Short History.* New York: Random House, 1957.

WINTER, YVOR. *In Defense of Reason*, 3rd ed. New York: Swallow, 1947.

WYCHERLEY, WILLIAM. *The Country Wife.* Ed. Thomas H. Fujimura. Lincoln: Univ. of Nebraska Press, 1965.

ZIMBARDO, ROSE A. *Wycherley's Drama: A Link in the Development of English Satire.* New Haven: Yale Univ. Press, 1965.

Index

Allen, Don Cameron, 146
All in the Family, 100
Aristophanes, 102
Aristotle, 15, 52–53, 55, 57, 64, 153
Arnold, Matthew, 55, 62–64, 154
Avery, Emmett L., 53, 150, 156

Babbitt, Irving, 155
Bate, Walter Jackson, 154
Bateson, F. W., x, 21, 22, 145
Beach, Richard, 161
Beljame, Alexandre, 6, 53
Bell, Daniel, 51
Berkeley, David S., 19
Birdsall, Virginia Ogden, 10, 17, 18, 98–99, 109
Bleich, David, 161
Bloomfield, Morton, 157
Bredvold, Louis, 155
Brooks, Cleanth, 152
Brown, Norman O., 13–14, 16–17, 97, 147
Bunker, Archie, 100–101
Burke, Edmund, 61
Burnim, Kalman, 161

Cassirer, Ernst, 154
Cecil, C. D., 15
Chaucer, Geoffrey, 79, 90, 95–96, 157

Cibber, Colley, 78
Cicero, 55
Collier, Jeremy, x, 1–3, 5, 9, 13, 16, 18, 23–25, 30–33, 39, 41–42, 53, 99, 140
Congreve, William, xiii, 3, 12, 23–24, 29–30, 35, 41, 46, 102
Crews, Frederick, 75

Dennis, John, xii, 23–27, 39
Dewey, John, 72
Dobrée, Bonamy, 42–46
Dryden, John, 3, 47, 55, 86, 150, 152
Duncan, Hugh Dalziel, 154
Durfey, Thomas, 85

Eliot, T. S., 7, 16, 56
Etherege, George, 12, 26, 40, 46

Fairholt, Frederick W., 157
Farce, 86, 88, 89
Farquhar, George, 35, 102
Feshbach, Seymour, 54
Fish, Stanley, 161
Freud, Sigmund, 13–17, 147
Frye, Northrop, 55–56, 115
Fujimura, Thomas H., 8, 12–13, 15–16, 18, 99, 109, 147, 158

175

Index

Gagen, Jean, 19
Gardner, John, 115
Garrick, David, 78
Ghosh, J. C., 159
Goodman, Paul, 97, 147
Gould, Jack, 158

Hagstrum, Jean H., 153, 159
Hamilton, Anthony, xi, 5
Hanzo, Thomas A., 153
Harbage, Alfred, 67
Harrington, Norman T., 157–58
Hawkins, Harriet, 78
Hazlitt, William, 35–36, 39, 41, 47, 49
Highfill, Philip, Jr., 161
Hirsch, E. D., Jr., 152, 156, 159
Hobbes, Thomas, 44
Hobson, Laura, 158
Holdsworth, Janet Nott, 154
Holland, Norman N., 12–13, 15–18, 69–71, 75, 99, 109, 146–47, 155, 161
Horace, 55, 153
Horner, Harry, 17, 22, 41, 98, 103. *See also* Wycherley, William
Hough, Graham, 154
Huizinga, John, 17
Hume, Robert D., xi, 78, 85–86, 89, 99, 102, 106, 109–10, 115, 125, 129, 138, 145–46, 150, 158, 160–61
Hunt, Leigh, 38–39
Hyman, Edgar, 155

Jeffares, Norman A., 157
Jonson, Ben, 52, 88, 137; *Volpone*, 95, 102

Kaufman, Anthony, 158
Kaul, Arnold, 7–8, 18
Kelly, Henry Ansgar, 157
Kenny, Shirley Strum, 160

King, Richard, 96, 147, 158
Kirsch, Arthur C., 150, 152
Knight, G. Wilson, 14, 16
Knights, L. C., 6, 7–8, 16, 33, 75
Kott, Jan, 13
Krieger, Murray, 150, 155
Krutch, Joseph Wood, 4, 146

Lamb, Charles, 13, 35–39, 41, 44–48, 109
Lane, Robert E., 66, 155
Langhans, Edward, 161
Laslett, Peter, xi, 145
Lear, Norman, 101
Leavis, F. R., 75
Lee, Nathaniel: *The Princess of Cleve*, 118
Legouis, Pierre, 10, 146
Lemon, Lee T., 155
Levin, Richard, 160
Lewis, C. S., 16
Longinus, 55
Love, Harold, 53, 150
Lovejoy, Arthur O., 61–62, 72
Lynch, Kathleen, 42, 45, 47–49

Macaulay, Thomas, x, 4, 6, 40, 53, 146
McDonald, Charles O., 28–30
Marks, Emerson R., 153
Miles, Dudley, 26–27, 30
Miner, Earl, x
Molière, 79, 88, 95–96
Montgomery, Guy, 20–21
Moore, Arthur K., 150
Moore, Frank Harper, 153

Nicoll, Allardyce, xi, 4, 6, 78, 90, 125, 146, 156

Olson, Paul A., 157
Otway, Thomas, 139, 159–60; *The Atheist*, xiii, 122–24; *The Souldiers Fortune*, 116–24

Index

Palmer, John, 26, 40–42, 44–45, 48, 64, 89, 99, 109, 150
Pepys, Samuel, xvii, 2, 5, 24
Perry, William G., Jr., 154
Plato, 53, 140
Pottle, Frederick A., 68, 155
Prynne, William, 1
Purves, Alan C., 161

Rahv, Philip, 72
Ravenscroft, Edward: *The London Cuckolds*, xiii, 76–97, 110, 112, 113, 115
Richards, I. A., 65, 71
Rieff, Philip, 147
Righter, William, 67, 72, 75, 156
Robertson, D. W., Jr., 79, 158
Robinson, Paul A., 147, 158
Rosenblatt, Louise, 161
Roszak, Theodore, 147

Sacks, Sheldon, 68–69
Santayana, George, x, 65, 145
Scheper, George L., 159
Schneider, Ben Ross, 30–33
Scouten, Arthur H., xi, 53, 125, 145, 150
Shadwell, Thomas: *The Squire of Alsatia*, xiii, 124–37; *The Virtuoso*, 118
Shaftesbury, Anthony Ashley Cooper, Earl of, 44, 72
Sherbo, Arthur H., 153
Sidney, Philip, 2, 55
Simon, Irène, 150
Singer, Roger, 54

Singh, Sarup, 47–49, 99, 150, 158
Smith, G. Gregory, 152
Smith, John Harrington, 153
Song of Solomon, 113
Southerne, Thomas: *The Wives Excuse*, 79, 86
Steele, Richard, xii, 25, 41, 78, 102
Summers, Montague, 157, 160
Sutherland, James, 78
Stoll, Elmer E., xii

Taine, H. A., 4, 6, 53, 146
Terence, 126–27
Tillyard, E. M. W., 52
Trumbo, Dalton, 154

Vanbrugh, John, 35
Van Lennep, William H., 158
Vernon, P. F., 21
Vivas, Eliseo, 150

Wain, John, x, 5, 146
Wallace, John, 161
Wellek, René, 61
Wilde, Oscar, xviii, 9, 41
Wilkinson, D. R. M., 19
Williams, Aubrey, 29–30, 159
Wimsatt, W. K., Jr., 152
Winters, Yvor, xvii, 16
Wycherley, William, xiii, 12, 35, 139; *The Country Wife*, 22, 76–77, 79, 89, 98–114

Zamora, Danny, 140
Zimbardo, Rose A., 99, 109
Zink, Sidney, 50, 65–66, 154

JOHN T. HARWOOD is an associate professor of English and director of the composition program at The Pennsylvania State University as well as a specialist in seventeenth- and eighteenth-century literature with a keen interest in the uses of criticism.

THE LIBRARY
ST. MARY'S COLLEGE OF MARYLAND
ST. MARY'S CITY, MARYLAND 20686